Postcolonial Studies in Education

Series Editors
Antonia Darder
Loyola Marymount University
Los Angeles, CA, USA

Anne Hickling-Hudson
Faculty of Education
Queensland University of Technology
Brisbane, Australia

Peter Mayo
Faculty of Education
University of Malta
Msida, Malta

Studies utilising the perspectives of postcolonial theory have become established and increasingly widespread in the last few decades. This series embraces and broadly employs the postcolonial approach. As a site of struggle, education has constituted a key vehicle for the 'colonization of the mind'. The 'post' in postcolonialism is both temporal, in the sense of emphasizing the processes of decolonization, and analytical in the sense of probing and contesting the aftermath of colonialism and the imperialism which succeeded it, utilising materialist and discourse analysis. Postcolonial theory is particularly apt for exploring the implications of educational colonialism, decolonization, experimentation, revisioning, contradiction and ambiguity not only for the former colonies, but also for the former colonial powers. This series views education as an important vehicle for both the inculcation and unlearning of colonial ideologies. It complements the diversity that exists in postcolonial studies of political economy, literature, sociology and the interdisciplinary domain of cultural studies. Education is here being viewed in its broadest contexts, and is not confined to institutionalized learning. The aim of this series is to identify and help establish new areas of educational inquiry in postcolonial studies.

More information about this series at
http://www.palgrave.com/gp/series/14536

Cueponcaxochitl D. Moreno Sandoval

Ancestral Knowledge Meets Computer Science Education

Environmental Change in Community

Cueponcaxochitl D. Moreno Sandoval
Native American and Mexican
Indigenous Studies, Ethnic Studies
Program
California State University, Stanislaus
Turlock, CA, USA

Postcolonial Studies in Education
ISBN 978-1-137-47519-0   ISBN 978-1-137-47520-6   (eBook)
https://doi.org/10.1057/978-1-137-47520-6

Library of Congress Control Number: 2019931928

Cover credit: © The Wall That Speaks, Sings, and Shouts by Paul Botello

This Palgrave Macmillan imprint is published by the registered company Springer Nature
America, Inc.
The registered company address is: 1 New York Plaza, New York, NY 10004, U.S.A.

To worldwide efforts in revitalizing ancestral knowledge systems towards a dignified and sustainable future for all.
And to our sun,
Cuixin.

ACKNOWLEDGEMENTS

I walk with thousands of ancestors inside me. Tlazohcamati to them and to many who have supported my work, my life, my being. To my husband, Tlazohtzin Ixtozohuani, for his availability and support, for being my biggest fan and a compassionate critic. To our precious sun, Cuixin Tlazohtzin, for inspiring me to be a better ancestor. To Suzanne and John Schaefer for their relentless encouragement and kinship. To the Anahuakenyxs and Urban Visionaries whose continuous inspiration colors the world of possibilities. To Xochimecayahualli and Nahuacalli for their continued guidance and relations. To my parents por sembrarme y a mis abuelitxs por cargarme. To my siblings, nieces and nephews whom I love. To my editor and friend, Maria Røst Winnie, for walking with me. Most definitely, to this little piece of earth I call home, La Florencita, tlazohcamati huei for nurturing our collective dreams. Xonahuiyacan.

CONTENTS

LIST OF FIGURES

List of Tables

CHAPTER 1

Uprooting Systems of Colonization: Naming Learning Ecologies as Eurocentric

Each chapter in this book details specific aspects of my career-long research, and explores concepts and intersections of interest in a way that invites dialogue, and attempts to interweave a detailed picture of where we came from and what we can grow toward.

In this work, you will be introduced to the concept of **Ancestral Computing (AC)**, which explores socio-cultural and -historical ecosystem approaches to solving complex problems. We are working toward social transformation, especially dismantling the remainders of colonialism all around us. Inherent in this system is the **coloniality of power**, a term popularized by Anibal Quijano, which speaks to lasting consequences of European colonialist practices. Evidence ranges from seemingly "inherent" social orders, to restriction of access to certain forms and methods of knowledge acquisition.

Next, we integrate what **el vivir comunitario**, or community wellness, entails, and how this path toward healing our communities with ancestral knowledge, healed and decolonized lifeways, and repairing the warped identities we inherited from forming our **identities under colonialism** leads to a brighter future for all.

At the end of this chapter, you will find an explanation of the study conducted in East Los Angeles, and further explanation of this book's structure. But first, a dedication and a setting of intent.

© The Author(s) 2019
C. D. M. Sandoval, *Ancestral Knowledge Meets Computer Science Education*, Postcolonial Studies in Education,
https://doi.org/10.1057/978-1-137-47520-6_1

We[1] acknowledge the Four Directions, beginning with our bodies turned to the direction where the rising sun peeks over the horizon. Our bare feet planted in the earth. We listen to the call of the concha as its vibrations penetrate through our skin. We rattle sonajas[2] and inhale the old smell of burning copal[3] as we colorfully move in unison to the ancient beat of the drum. We acknowledge and ask permission to the old guardians of the land we stand on to begin participatory research as ceremony so that this work continues to nurture el vivir comunitario (or communal wellness[4]) with a focus on educational excellence in AC for sustainability. We tie ourselves to this place[5] and nurture its sanctity as we continue our journey toward educational excellence, even in the face of disdain. In a time when restrictive policies manifest present-day colonialism in our public schooling systems, when these colonialist ideologies and practices attempt to dismantle our collective dignities, we brace ourselves. We feel gratitude for the work that has led us here and we spiritually and mentally prepare for the work ahead of us.

In *Buen Vivir / Vivir Bien Filosofía, políticas, estrategias y experiencias regionales andinas,* Fernando Huanacuni Mamani writes how a people "who march toward their liberation" with dignity and sovereignty is unstoppable. May the voice of time and Mother Earth accompany us on this journey.

La cultura cura[6]—literally meaning "the culture[7] cures" and, by extension, "the old ways of our ancestors will help us heal"—is a common invocation drawn by a narrative that, in this book, is rooted in the ancestral knowledge of the Mexicayotl, an old way of understanding and practicing ancestral knowledge systems that originated from Mexico. While some scholars have suggested that the Mexicayotl is a form of religion, I respectfully disagree. Like many other English terms in this book, fitting a religious category to describe the Mexicayotl is like fitting a square into a circle, or comparing apples and oranges; it is nearly impossible because the worldviews are incomparable. For example, one of the main areas of non-comparison is the lack of a centralized governing body in the Mexicayotl, as opposed to religious sectors that have organized governing bodies. This query sets the tone for this book as the narrative that brings together ancestral knowledge and computer science education, two seemingly disparate bodies of knowledge. Ancestral knowledge systems, for the scope of this book, are rooted in the ancestral foodways of the Mexicayotl across the ecologies of teaching and learning, a student-led organization named Movimiento Estudiantil Chican@s de Aztlan (MEChA), a computer science course, and a larger schooling community that included multiple circles of participation. Through these complex ecologies, we will follow Itzel, a high school junior at the time of the beginning of this critical narrative inquiry.

There are various layers of complexity that go along with two traditions that stem from two different language roots, worldviews, knowledge systems. Unfortunately, as religion is one of those, Religion is defined by the Oxford Dictionary (2015) as a Mesoamerican[8] (Kirchhoff, 1943) cultural practices to resist neoliberalism in schools under the coloniality of power[9] (Quijano, 2000). This book reveals living Mesoamerican AC[10] practices as an asset-based approach to teaching and learning within a student-led organization, a CS classroom and a larger schooling community of El Sereno.

At its core, this book is an historical document that speaks back to the dominant European epistemology of urban schools. I unearth the cultural practices of Mesoamerican-descent populations as academic practices while addressing the disequilibrium of social and material value placed on the historical epistemologies of Mesoamerican-descent peoples in one comprehensive public high school of El Sereno. This Narrative Inquiry follows the academic voice of a mestiza consciousness (Anzaldúa, 1987) exposing non-Eurocentric academic practices, such that a plurality of knowledge systems is reinforced. For example, I "write bilingually and...switch codes without having always to translate...using my serpent's tongue...overcom[ing] the tradition of silence." (Anzaldúa, 1987) Because of the non-Eurocentric academic approach, you may find that reading this research elicits an emotional response. I respectfully ask that you experience that emotion and reflect on it as part of the journey toward decolonizing[11] educational practices, ya que "pa' todo hay remedio, menos la muerte."[12] I have included several endnotes as a guide to the alterative model (Grosfoguel, 2008) I present in this book. The number of endnotes does not "justify" my position, rather, end-noting is used here to scaffold the learning and engagement of those who may not be familiar with a mestiza consciousness and who are open to becoming familiar with a native-to-the-Western-hemisphere epistemological approach within this schooling community.

The purpose of this participatory action research is to explore an approach and effect that exposes the socio-cultural and -historical wealth of a community of practice as it bridges a positive academic cultural identity in learning and collective agency in a student-led organization, a computer science classroom and larger schooling community at an urban high school in Los Angeles on a path toward general educational excellence and wellness. Each of these organizational structures is described through the participation of Itzel,[13] a junior at Lomas High School in 2009 who weaved these structures over three years. This path moves away from the colonizing paradigm that dominates the way we generally conceptualize such situations. In our everyday lived experience, there is an unforgiving momentum to adopt ways of being that are Eurocentric within a coloniality of power, especially in schools. This work is about unearthing the AC of a community's cultural wealth (Yosso & Solórzano, 2006) as a dialectical theory.[14] In exposing the long legacy of the cultural assets of this community of practice, we are careful to be critical of our own predispositions, thereby avoiding falling into another yet Eurocentric perspective, which romanticizes, essentializes, and exoticizies a culture as "the other" by looking at it through a foreign gaze. Yet it is impossible to delineate what is Eurocentric and what is not as the lines are not so easily clear-cut and we do not fit a nicely organized binary of opposites. Similarly, we cannot place ourselves in solely Mesoamerican practices because it is impossible to avoid interactions with neoliberalism. Yet this book exposes a process that complicates and challenges the often-taken-for-granted monolithic approach to living, learning, and dying. We draw upon socio-historical ways of exposing the *process* of a culture, which is not static, monolithic, or two-dimensional. Instead, we (re)discover assets that have been passed on to us by the elders in our families and communities as principal knowledge-keepers. In addition, we walk toward learning more about our own ways, by making yearly pilgrimages to Mexico[15] to read our ancient books and plant our feet on our ancient structures with careful and critical minds, and by studying our anthropological works. Through our work to form our own cultural identities from the ground up, we seek to act critically for sustainable and equitable educational excellence as we (re)develop healthy families and a healthy community. This work zeroes in on the way in which a CS classroom with a teacher, whose background does not reflect the cultural history of his students, experiences this vision and action.

My father once told my siblings and me after the first purchase of a computer for our home, "Yo quiero que aprendan de las computadoras porque esas van a apoderarse del mundo algún día[16]." I was a sophomore in high school. Our parents saved up years of recycling glass and plastic bottles con tanto sacrificio to purchase a computer so that my siblings and I would be well equipped to do our homework assignments that required computerized text. My brother, the eldest, soon "took over" the keyboard to punch away yellow text on a black screen. Although I was intrigued by the nuances of this new tool at our disposal, I feared that if I pushed the wrong button, the computer would break. My curiosity, however, led me to dabble with the keyboard to learn the basics of typing and playing solitaire.

Fast-forward almost two decades and I was positioned as an educational researcher to broaden participation in computing through a National Science Foundation initiative whose mission was to democratize computer science by including the participation of underrepresented cultural groups in computing, especially females. My training in critical theory and pedagogy has equipped me with the focus on the social analysis of this field as an issue in equity, not a technical focus on computer science. This book demystifies the common assumption that computers presume greater power than our human agency, particularly in non-dominant populations.

1.1   Statement of the Problem: "If We Don't Know Our History, How Can We Imagine Our Future?"[17]

Even though the fastest growing population in the United States is of Mesoamerican or Anahuac descent,[18] there is no clear pathway to educational excellence para el vivir comunitario[19] as part of the nation's agenda. Instead, we are bearing witness to present-day colonialism in a racially stratified society (Omi & Winant, 1974) that operates under punitive high-stakes measures to "correct" the "academic gap" as a reactionary approach to teaching and learning. Unlike European-origin immigrants like Italians and many Jews, the Mesoamerican-descent school-age population is consistently underachieving academically at high rates, and this group remains the most undereducated major population group in the country (Gándara & Contreras, 2009). Instead of a holistic approach to el vivir comunitario, this group consistently encounters negative stereotypes and is systematically denied entrance to our own original cultural identities as academic practices. In a racially structured society, this population does not have an equal opportunity to meet the most basic human needs, let alone to routinely contribute to knowledge (re)production.[20] This is particularly salient in a field that inextricably shapes our lives, computer science, which is one of the most segregated in education (Goode, 2007; Margolis, Estrella, Goode, 2008). Instead, Native peoples of the Western Hemisphere are forcibly crammed into an ever-present colonial practice that seeks to homogenize our practices into English-only language, capitalist consumerism, and patriarchal individualism, ripping us away from our ancestral praxis. The colonization of the land and peoples by a Eurocentric world power is far from over (Bonilla-Silva, 2001; Churchill, 1994; McLaren, 2007; Omi & Winant, 1974). Until we learn to decolonize[21] ourselves as a collective, any societal solution we reach will remain only partial.

1.1.1   Identity Formation Under Colonialism

The public schooling system as a social institution reflects a long historical process of a hierarchical classification of peoples, which began with the constitution of America and world capitalism as a Euro-centered colonial/modern world power (Grosfoguel, 2004; Quijano, 2000). The establishment of this world power entailed the imposition and reproduction of a socially structured idea of race, "a mental construct that expresses colonial experience and that pervades the most important dimensions of world power, including its specific rationality: Eurocentrism" (Quijano, 2000, p. 215). This is often enforced through racial projects—"an interpretation, representation, or explanation of racial dynamics, and an effort to reorganize and redistribute resources along particular racial lines" (Omi & Winant, 1974, p. 56). The idea of "race" as biologically structured and hierarchical "was not meant to explain just the external or physiognomic differences between the dominant and the dominated, but also the mental and cultural differences" (Quijano, 2000, p. 216). In addition, the pervasive ideology around the "cultural representation" (Omi & Winant, 1994, p. 66) of race reproduces the hegemonic structure of the coloniality of power (Quijano, 1991, 1998) or *el patrón del poder colonial* (McLaren, personal communication, July 30, 2011), which continues a living legacy of colonialism via racial, sexual, spiritual, legal, political, economic, and social hierarchical orders imposed by European colonialism that pervades our current approaches to being in the world.

This unequal distribution of world power penetrates the public schooling system, particularly in urban schools. People of color experience a systematic denial of academic rigor, excellence, and wellness in classrooms and schools. Coloniality of power is ever-so-present in legislation and through the lack of opportunities in both curricular projects and in the educational system based on the idea of race[22] that perpetuates the legislative hegemonic actions, described by Omi and Winant as racial projects. These racial projects (Omi & Winant, 1974) perpetuate a legacy of group disparities. For example, Arizona's SB 2281 banned the original cultural knowledge systems taught in schools under the auspices that this knowledge would "advocate ethnic solidarity instead of the treatment of pupils as individuals," etc. This legislation is a clear example of a racial project that pushes for a systematic denial of access to the original history of these lands and the people that tend to it on a daily basis. At its liver center,[23] this book challenges epistemological traditions historically enforced by public schooling institutions.

Groups with a long history of colonial relations with an imperial state are particularly vulnerable to negative representations of their identities (Grosfoguel, 2004). What is considered knowledge, and what kind of knowledge is valid? The Eurocentric concept of "knowing" rests on an approach to rational knowledge that references a specific historical experience that considers all non-European peoples "objects" of knowledge. This objectification produces hegemony that dictates social institutional relations without questioning a pervasive ideology. A coloniality of power names the continuities in the relationships of exploitation and domination between Westerners and non-Westerners that have been built during centuries of European colonial expansion, with an emphasis on cultural and social power relations (Grosfoguel, 2004, p. 325). As Grosfoguel (2004) noted, "These ideas have configured a deep and persistent cultural formation that is reflected by a matrix of ideas, images, values, attitudes, and social practices, that do not cease to be implicated in relationships among people" (p. 326). National ideologies lead us to an unjust distribution of power. This creates dehumanizing practices that stifle creativity, particularly in K-12 science education (Barrow, 2010; Johnston, 2007; Rennera, Brown, Stiens, & Burton, 2010) and in urban centers, where power relations and practices are magnified (Anyon, 1997). The international movement to Occupy Wall Street (that began in 2011) demonstrated a high level of discontent regarding corporate greed and war-mongering behavior, among other issues.

Overlapped with racial constructions, urban schools reflect a factory model that reproduces a division of labor designed to sustain economic imbalance[24] (Bowles & Gintis, 1976; Tyack, 1974). And there's no better context in which to reproduce an economic system than public schools to reinforce a standard disequilibrium of power, especially in computer science (more on this in Chapter 2). It comes as no surprise, then, that only an estimated 68% of Mesoamerican-descent students who enter the 9th grade graduate from high school with a regular diploma in the 12th grade and that, in 2001, only 50% of all African American students, 51% of Native American students, and 53% of all Mesoamerican students graduated from high school. These rates are significantly lower than the national average. If we look only at males, we see that they fare even worse, at 43, 47, and 48% respectively (Orfield, Losen, Wald, & Swanson, 2004).

Moreover, urban students who attend public schools are often conditioned to "divorce ourselves from ourselves" (Morrell, personal communication, November 24, 2008) so that we "fit" into a dominant status quo that follows the legacy of a coloniality of power. The effects are profound, and they have to do with the way we think of ourselves when we look at ourselves in the mirror. As history continues to unfold, non-dominant groups find ourselves operating within a colonizing framework and looking at ourselves with a distorted mirror in which our resistive agency and colonial forces—internal and external—clash:

> The tragedy is that we all have been led, knowingly or not, willingly or not, to see and to accept that image as our own reality. Because of it, for a very long time we have been what we are not, what we never should have been and what we never will be. And because of it we can never catch our real problems, much less solve them, except in only a partial or distorted way. (Quijano, 2000, p. 222)

At its core, this book challenges the Eurocentric model of knowledge (re)production that is founded on the continued coloniality of power that is coded as racial projects today. This is particularly the case in computer science, a field that inextricably shapes the way we interact socially with the world, and which constitutes one of the most segregated subjects in education (Margolis et al., 2008). Only one of every ten students who graduated with a computer science degree in 2008–2009 was African American, Mesoamerican-descent, or Native American (Goode, 2007). For these general reasons, we look toward developing positive cultural and academic identities through the development of a critical awareness of the historical forces of colonization, even in computer science.

Schooling practices reflect a systemic colonization process on a larger scale. Particularly, Richard Kahn (2010) critically examines the uses of technology and mainstream media in the interest of the neoliberal marketplace as it promotes a hierarchy in labor production. Moreover, curriculum and instruction within STEM[25] and computing fields has historically been devoid of the community cultural wealth of disenfranchised groups (Eglash, 2001; Moreno Sandoval, 2017). Instead of rejecting technology in its totality, as Jerry Mander (1992) suggested for the survival of indigenous nations, Eglash proposed that researchers look to the rich ancestral praxis systems that live historically in the indigenous practices of students' community cultural wealth as "a potential source for changes in reconstructing identity, social position, and access to power" (Eglash, 2001, p. 353). Although Eglash does not provide a critique of the context in which he presents ancestral knowledges and practices, nor does he inform us about his positionality in studying "the other," Eglash provides a space to engage the intellectual contributions of indigenous peoples throughout the world through his use of culturally situated design tools. His approach looks at historical and current practices of disenfranchised groups and brings to light the intellectual contributions of these civilizations through art and architectural designs among other ways.

Similarly, Tara Yosso (2005) called on stakeholders to develop schools that acknowledge the multiple strengths of communities of color, shifting away from deficit views that capitalize on a culture of poverty or considering culture as "disabilities" and that these disabilities are clear fabrications of the "power of culture [itself] to disable" (McDermott & Varenne, 1995, p. 327). Curricula can and should engage the array of cultural knowledge, skills, and abilities diverse students bring from their communities into the classroom. Danny Martin's (2000, 2007, 2009a, 2009b) work in mathematics education shows that African American students' identities and agencies are affected by their (non)participation in mathematics education. He argues that "life experience as an African American, often characterized by struggle and social devaluation, makes it difficult to maintain a positive identity in the pursuit of mathematics knowledge" (2007, p. 157).

As a non-dominant cultural group that faces the coloniality of power, the participants in this study, who are part of a schooling community of El Sereno, act in solidarity with other oppressed groups. For this reason, we come together as a counter-culture[26] to combat—both silently and vociferously, both subliminally and forcefully—the forces of disequilibrium of power. We bring forth an "oppositional consciousness" (Sandoval, 2000) that serves to dismantle the structures of power that are embedded in our daily struggle to survive. We draw from our ancestral praxis to reclaim our power as a community highlighting what Kahn (2010) calls an ecopedagogical praxis that is "shaped by the power of human emotions, the cultural rituals of diverse ways of being, a deep respect for universal rights, and the integration of planetary consciousness" (p. xvi). We use our imagination to create spaces that honor and hold our dignity intact as an alterative revolutionary practice that Grace Lee Boggs and Angela Davis presented about during the twenty-seventh annual empowering woman of color conference in Berkeley, CA.

1.2   Explanation of the Study

This work is grounded within a socio-historical and -cultural analysis of the current state of urban schooling in the United States, beginning with the lens offered by Quijano (2000). We first apply his historical analysis of racialization in America since the colonization by Europeans, and we later utilize his description of a coloniality of power that pervades our current social system. Since schooling practices mirror social politics in this country, it is useful to frame our analysis within this lens, as we will later provide an alternative that works through and out of this disleveled economic system.

Next, we look at urban schools within a larger matrix of "gendered and racialized positionalities driven by power-sensitive and power-expansive relations of symmetrical privilege, and in a social space aligned and vectored geopolitically and cross-hatched socioculturally..." (Conversation with McLaren by Sebastjan Leban, 2010, part 1). This totalizing of power and capital has created an overarching matrix of exploitation that generates unequal distributions of power. Breaking free from the coloniality of power (Quijano, 2000) that encapsulates urban schools is not a simple crossing. To explore the nuances of critique and opportunity, I study a three-year journey of positive identity formation and collective agency by leveraging AC practices in three organizational structures that are connected by the participation of Itzel, a high school junior in 2009.

Drawing from western-hemisphere indigenous epistemology, this empirical research study challenges Eurocentric notions of knowledge (re)production found in institutional ivory towers of world power. However, I do not choose to reject European knowledge in its totality. This challenge is enacted through selectively and unapologetically drawing from both European and non-Western epistemological ways of knowing as a way to speak to larger audiences that are familiar with any or all of these knowledge systems. This book foregrounds its methodological approach by drawing on a Xicana Sacred Space[27] (XSS) that strategically interweaves a multiplicity of approaches to scholarship. XSS centers on native knowledge systems of the Western hemisphere, while still drawing on European notions in scholarship, simultaneously and without any sense of compromise.

Similarly, this framework draws on Narrative Inquiry methodology in that it utilizes participatory action research in spatial, temporal, and social commonplace by narrating the epistemic approach to making sense of individual and collective identity formation and agency, one that has been particularly absent in science education research (Barton and Tobin, 2001; Behar, 1996). A XSS also draws on Vygotskian socio-historical notions of development, which "describe learning and change as the internalization and transformation of cultural tools that occur as individuals participate in social practice" (Gallucci et al., 2010, p. 547). This methodological approach affords an analysis that frames community cultural wealth (Yosso, 2005), focusing particularly on ancestral praxis and computing as a figured world that promotes critical identity formation and leveraging agency using digital technology (Holland & Lachiotte 1998). This conceptual framework is helpful in that it provides a means to conceptualize "*historical* subjectivities, consciousness, and agency and persons (and collective agents) forming in practice" (Holland & Lachiotte 1998, p. 41). Subsequently, this Vygotskian model helps frame the journey of a high school student of Mesoamerican descent, Itzel, as she travels through various figured worlds within the schooling spatial context of El Sereno.

I explore the building of a figured world of AC as it provides a positive learning ecology that draws upon a community's historical cultural assets as an academic practice in formal and informal spaces that include a student-led organization that meets on and off campus, a CS classroom and in school-wide spaces that may provide a context for challenging and engaging in digital tool production. This study proffers the capacity to bridge the gap between CS and community cultural practices.

My participation and activism in this study is grounded in a XSS (Diaz-Soto, Soon, Villarreal, & Campos, 2009) that prioritizes my cultural intuition (Delgado Bernal, 1998) and ancestral knowledge systems (Moreno Sandoval, Mojica Lagunas, Montelongo, & Díaz, 2016) as a classroom researcher who is also an El Sereno resident and a scholar activist of Mesoamerican descent. Through my unique participation, which dovetails with the lived experiences of the communities in which we serve, I focus on remembering our ancestral knowledge systems as a way to restore our collective dignity in academic and social spaces. As a participant observer on three levels of the organization, with a small thread of auto-ethnographic connections, I weave the pre-existing cultural practices of our community into one CS high school urban classroom of El Sereno.

From a Grounded Theory approach, and over the course of three academic years, I have collected qualitative data on three organizational levels to track the ways in which situated action (Vaughan, 2002) can affect organizational change over time. Vaughan's (2002) research examines the "linkage between environment, organizations, and individual action and meaning" (p. 2). These three levels of organization have shaped the three findings chapters that illustrate the complexity and intricacy of colonizing and decolonizing practices as encapsulated in three embedded spaces—a student-led organization, a CS classroom, and a schooling community. In this critical ethnographic case study, I look at El Sereno as a physical space that exists as one of the 272 neighborhoods of one of the most populated cities in the world by Mexican-descent peoples: Los Angeles. The ecological neighborhood of El Sereno sets the stage for its schools. Thus, the schooling community of Lomas High School is analyzed as the macro-level of this study. At Lomas High School, I focus on a student-led organization, a computer science classroom, and the greater schooling community that encompasses a Parent Center and a teacher-initiated interdisciplinary collective. I laser in on ways in which a community's cultural wealth informs teaching and learning in a computer science classroom with a teacher whose background does not reflect the cultural heritage of his students. Although the context of the neighborhood and school I present here is important, the greater part of my focus and analysis takes place in the CS high school classroom, as I follow Itzel's process of telling identities and action in and outside the classroom space. Particular attention was given to the teacher's development of critical academic and "cultural competence" (Milner, 2011) as he strove to meet the needs of his students. With this aim, he participated and collaborated with a group of interdisciplinary teachers to mobilize ancestral memory, advanced technology, and student inquiry for health in an El Sereno schooling community.

The approach of this book mirrors the ebb and flow of a modern accordion, contracting and expanding over space and time. If you listen closely for long enough, you can sense the beat of an ancient drum.[28]

1.3 Scholarly Significance

The scholarly significance of this work is three-fold; it: (1) reveals how ancestral praxis may be leveraged (even as a contested space) to form positive identities in and beyond computer science classrooms; (2) provides a framework that spawns a decolonizing culture for collective agency toward wellness and educational excellence; and (3) illustrates a method that bridges student-led initiatives to classroom practice and neighborhood-wide spaces.

In essence, I propose to uncover the richness of our ancestral praxis systems while connecting them to the questioning and appropriation of digital science production. The collective practice of remembering our ancient Caxcan, Cora, Huichol, Zapoteco, Raramuri, for example, cultural practices of Mesoamerica within the innumerability of diversity (Paris, 2012) may help us imagine something new (Martínez, 2009). Although it is not enough to simply remember and imagine, this is the first step to developing a common purpose and creating something sustainable for ourselves and our environment.

1.4 Research Questions

Through this study, I explore the following central question: **How may Mesoamerican academic cultural practices provide a foundation for a positive learning ecology of cultural academic identities in three organizational levels of a public high school, especially in spaces that have been historically segregated, like computer science education?**

The following three organizational clusters of sub-questions help guide the focus of my data collection, analysis, and discussion:

1. *Informal microlevel: Student-led high school organization*
   How may student inquiry co-influence positive collective identities and agencies for communal wellness, including educational excellence?
2. *Formal meso-level: CS classroom*
   How do participants make sense of and act on ancestral praxis and computer science intersections over time?
3. *Formal and informal macro-level: Cross-campus neighborhood schooling community*
   How may student-led initiatives and classroom practices inform a neighborhood-wide schooling movement para el vivir comunitario, including educational excellence?

1.5   STRUCTURE OF THIS BOOK

This Narrative Inquiry includes a participatory action research approach that offers a space to conduct and present research grounded in the knowledge of Mexican-descent peoples. Data were gathered from classroom participant observations, and student and teacher gatherings. Coding focused on student engagement and the inclusion of community cultural practices in the CS classroom. Preliminary findings show that students' interest in CS was enhanced when the curriculum was tied to projects that were meaningful to the North-East Los Angeles community.

Chapter 2 includes a literature review and the theoretical framework followed in this Narrative Inquiry. I begin with a historical discussion about the evolution of Mexican-descent peoples in the United States under the coloniality of power. I offer the development of ancestral praxis systems as a tool for decolonizing our identities by returning to our cultural home.[29] I then review the literature at the intersection of ancestral praxis and computer science. Finally, I end with a review of learning as an agent of communal wellness in a schooling community.

Chapter 3 records a methodology that draws upon non-Eurocentric epistemology. It begins with a discussion of an indigenous research paradigm that includes the use of Narrative Inquiry to guide the approach to my research design and the analysis of my data. This chapter also details the data collection as it relates to my central and secondary questions. I describe the narrative in a three-level process that begins with the action research of participating in a student-led high school organization and witnessing the development of campus-wide student inquiry projects. Then, I study the meso (CS classroom) and macro (El Sereno Schooling Community) as sites where AP and CS learning serve as tools for positive identity formation and agency in a path toward communal wellness. I justify my data collection methods through a Grounded Theory approach, and I match my sources of information with the questions I aim to explore. I end with a discussion of the limitations of this study.

Chapter 4 will serve to ground the study within the knowledge systems that students and others in the organization blend to affect the collective formation of cultural and academic identities at the school level. This chapter focuses on Itzel, a junior in 2009–2010, who follows her friend's advice to join a student-led organization on campus, MEChA.[30] This chapter will delineate how she chose to participate at the microlevel of the schooling organizational structure, which is campus-wide. In addition, the knowledge revealed during this academic year will be leveraged, as this student models academic and deep cultural identities in the CS classroom during the subsequent academic year.

Chapter 5 focuses on the CS classroom in which Itzel enrolls for the second full academic year (2010–2011). During this time, she maintains her leadership in MEChA. Upon graduating from Lomas HS, Itzel enrolls at the University of California and declares Communications as her major and Computer Science as her minor area of focus. This chapter analyzes student artifacts and reflections, as well as the teacher's participation in the classroom and his reflections on cultural and content learning. Both AP and CS will be examined through identity formation and CS learning for agency in communal wellness.

Chapter 6 looks at the macro-level of a schooling community that includes Itzel, the CS teacher, an interdisciplinary team of teachers, and a non-profit organization that leads cross-campus-wide efforts to build communal wellness. Community-wide themes of identity formation and agency are analyzed and connected to the meso- and micro-levels of participation among a group of students who started out by seeking: (a) cultural awareness, (b) connections to the community, and (c) higher education. Implications for educational researchers, high school students, educators, and university stakeholders follow.

The nuances that are presented in this book follow the inquiries of a small student group who sought to promote cultural awareness across their public high school campus. Not surprising, ancestral cultural awareness is one of my passions, so when Mr. Floragon asked me to sponsor this organization, me calló como anillo al dedo. I did not know it then, but my participation in this student-led organization formed the foundation for this three-year research study. Simultaneously, I joined the Exploring Computer Science team, a National Science Foundation-funded project to broaden participation in computing. At the time, it was a job that paid the bills, but as I continued with the project and learned more about the racial disparities in this area, I became more critical about the positioning of computing. I raised many questions to various communities of practice that I belong to, including my family and friends, a Mesoamerican study group and an elder's circle. I time-traveled to the first time I interacted with a computer. My parents sacrificed so much to bring a computer home for my siblings and I to "aprender de lo que va a apoderar al mundo un día."

NOTES

1. Throughout this study, I will use "we" to speak on behalf of a schooling community that worked together over three years, with whom I've had the privilege to participate. I take full responsibility for the representations presented here of our work together.
2. A musical instrument usually made of dried gourds and seeds, a rattle.
3. A transparent resin made from tree sap. It is commonly used as incense both in ritual and everyday life.
4. In this study, "communal wellness" is defined as the fluid positive condition of physical, spiritual, emotional, and intellectual/creative health, especially when maintained by positive habits. My grandmother would say, "Mira que chapeteado está y es muy alegre." One's color in the face and mood help indicate a state of wellness, by the elder's observations.
5. For further explanation on sacred space and ceremony as they are used in this study, refer to Chapter 3.
6. The phrase was made popular by José Antonio Burciaga's (1992) publication, *Drink Cultura*.
7. This Narrative Inquiry draws from Cobb and Hodge's (2007) working definition of *culture* as a dialectical relationship between two views: "In one view, culture is treated as a characteristic of readily identified and thus circumscribable communities, whereas in the other views it is treated as a set of locally instantiated practices that are dynamic and improvisational" (p. 159). This non-static view of culture that "brings the identities and interests that students develop in mathematics classrooms to the fore make it directly available to researchers who focus on instructional design, learning, and teaching at the classroom level" (p. 159).

In addition, Holland and Lachiotte (1998) substantiated that culture needs to move more solidly into process and must be "predicated upon continuing cultural production: a development, or interlocking genesis, that is actually a co-development of identities, discourses, embodiments, and imagined worlds that inform each moment of joint production and are themselves transformed by that moment" (p. vii).

8. Mesoamerica, a protagonist of this story, interacts with temporal and spatial commonplaces, a social landscape of cultural practices that are rooted in an historical operation. Spatially, Mesoamerica extends from Northern México to Honduras and spans over 3500 years of documented history. In this book, Mesoamerican historical cultural practices are analytically perceived as a Figured World (Holland & Lachiotte 1998) that is socially constructed for an approach to social academic healing in a public urban high school. A further discussion of Mesoamerica can be found in Chapter 2.

9. The coloniality of power is a system that exposes the systems of domination in present-day colonialism connected to the disempowerment of non-dominant groups that are native-to-the-Western-Hemisphere. See Chapter 2 for a further discussion on the coloniality of power, specifically in public schools.

10. AC is described in Chapter 2.

11. In this book, I use Darder's (2012) notion of decolonizing sexual politics as a critique of critical pedagogy by feminist scholars. This approach challenges patriarchal discourses of power under the scope of critical theory such as "technocratic rationality, instrumentalism, efficiency, objectivity, and a privileging of the cognitive domain in the production of knowledge." (p. 98) At its heart, a decolonizing practice would challenge the coloniality of power by including "personal biography, narratives, a rethinking of authority, and an explicit engagement with the historical and political location of the knowing subject" (p. 98)

12. 'There is a solution to everything, except death.' This is a *dicho*, a saying, that my paternal grandmother shares with us, our family in El Sereno.

13. Participants and school name are replaced with pseudonyms.

14. A dialectical theory (Darder, 2012) is an approach that recognizes the contradictions inherent in the worlds of human existence. Under critical pedagogy, Darder (2012) cites Peter McLaren (1988) in that people are "essentially unfree and inhabit a world rife with contradictions and asymmetries of power and privilege...the problems of society [are] more than simply isolated events of individuals or deficiencies in the social structure..." (p. 166).

15. See http://www.youtube.com/watch?v=pSpWZ7BRq1s&feature=plcp.

16. I want you to learn about computers because in the future, they will take over.

17. Statement by Lomas High School Movimiento Estudiantil Chican@s de Aztlán (Lomas High School MEChA) student during a board meeting at a nearby McDonald's restaurant on January 11, 2011.

18. *Anahuac-descent* is a Nahuatl term used to describe people from Anahuac. Anahuac is a conjunction of two words *atl*—meaning 'water' (Karttunen, 1992, p. 13)—and *nahuac*—meaning 'adjacent to' (Karttunen, 1992, p. 157)—so *Anahuac* can be interpreted as 'next to the water' and by extension, as the Central Valley of Tenochtitlan, Mexico. This book includes Mexican and Central American groups as of Mesoamerican-descent, but focus is given to Mexican-descent peoples, who comprising two-thirds of Mesoamerican-descent people in the United States (Gandara & Contreras, 2009). In addition, Nahuatl is an original language of the Western Hemisphere, a derivative of the Uto-Aztecan root, so it is given importance in this research as one of the original languages of this Western continent. The Mexica Movement uses *nican tlaca* as a term that identifies all people with native ancestry on the western hemisphere, meaning "we are here". I use *Mesoamerican-descent peoples* mostly is used as a term that points to a counter-narrative that posits Eurocentric terms like Latino and Hispanic (commonly used as identifiers imposed on us) against the backdrop of colonialism. However, I use *Mesoamerican-descent peoples* as a term within a contested space that does not intend to *glorify* indigenous knowledge as utopia. Indeed, human interactions have included some flavor of colonizing practices both before and after European contact. And although the Yuto-Aztecan root influences languages throughout the hemisphere, Nahuatl is not historically spoken by native groups of the northern hemisphere, so, in essence, my use of the term here is within a contested space of knowledges. I use it to point to knowledge systems that have been documented in this continent for millennia as a way to promote a multiplicity of knowledges today. For further discussion on the (r)EVOLution of identity for Mesoamerican-descent peoples, refer to Chapter 2.

19. El buen vivir (Huanacuni Mamani, 2010) comunitario is a process that resonates in places in the southern part of the Western Hemisphere. The process indicates a communal approach to return to our ancestral roots for a model that may inform our current political, economic and social well-being. However, I choose to simply state "el vivir comunitario" to include a dialectical approach to living, learning and dying that is not romanticized as "buen" or "good", a false binary of opposites (as opposed to "mal" or "bad") as if each side "good/bad" exists in isolation of its opposite. Instead, to include el vivir comunitario prefers a sustainable democratic approach to living interdependently with one another and our environment with the common notion that 'no hay mal que

por bien no venga' or an approach that embraces the commonly invo-
cated Ometeotl that embraces duality such as sunrise/sunset, young/old,
beginning/end as a process that accepts all variations of life as they are. It
is up to us to evaluate and collectively create what we imagine is possible
for living inter-dependently with other peoples/animals and the cycles of
the natural world. Turn to Chapter 2 for a deeper discussion on el vivir
comunitario and ancestral praxis.

20. (Re)production is used against the notion that knowledge is owned by
individuals and that ideas are thus reproduced over time. The use of
(re) in parenthesis in this book reminds us that knowledge production is
recursive.

21. Refer to Chapter 2 for a further explanation of *decolonization* as it is used
in this study.

22. For a further explanation of racialization process, refer to Chapter 2.

23. Medicine in Mesoamerican historical practices include the liver as one
of the three vital organs that must operate harmoniously for a person
to be sane and mentally balanced. The functions of the heart and liver
have an intimate relationship that corresponds with one another. The
liver is associated with a nighttime sun which travels inside the earth; it
is also a blood rich organ necessary for thinking (Viesca, 2003; López-
Austin, 1980).

24. For a further discussion on economic interactions within the context of
public schooling, refer to Chapter 2.

25. Science, Technology, Engineering, and Mathematics

26. The term "counter-culture" refers to a decolonial practice of knowing
and acting in the world that moves away from a coloniality of power and
toward communal wellness, which includes positive intellectual and cultural identities.

27. For a more detailed explanation of XSS, refer to Chapter 3.

28. The modern version of the accordion originates in Germany and is widely
used in today's Mexican musical culture as an adaptation of European
influences. However, the sound of the huehuetl, the old drum, carries the
historical roots of Mesoamerica.

29. With *home*, I am referring to a spiritual, psychological, physical, and intellectual space that does not necessarily equate with a geographical region.

30. MEChA is an acronym for Movimiento Estudiantil Chican@s de Aztlan,
translated as 'Chican@ Student Movement of Aztlan,' a national organization that was born of the Civil Rights Movement with the creation
of El Plan de Santa Barbara, a manifesto that details a plan for equitable education and human rights for Chican@ students. The word Spanish
mecha means 'fuse,' and the motto of over 400 chapters nationwide of
MEChA is *La unión hace la fuerza*, or 'Unity makes strength.'

REFERENCES

Anyon, J. (1997). *Ghetto schooling: A political economy of urban educational reform.* New York: Teachers College Press, Teachers College, Columbia University.

Anzaldúa, G. E. (1987). *Borderlands/La Frontera: The New Mestiza.* San Francisco: Aunt Lute Books.

Barrow, L. H. (2010). Encouraging creativity with scientific inquiry. *Creative Education, 1*(1), 1–6.

Barton, A. C., & Tobin, K. (2001). Urban science education. *Journal of Research in Science Teaching, 38*, 843–846.

Behar, R. (1996). *The vulnerable observer: Anthropology that breaks your heart.* Boston, MA: Beacon Press.

Bonilla-Silva, E. (2001). *White supremacy and racism in the post-civil rights era,* Lynne. Boulder, CO: Rienner.

Bowles, S., & Gintis, H. (1976). *Schooling in capitalist America: Educational reform and the contradictions of economic life.* New York: Basic Books.

Burciaga, J. A. (1992). *Drink cultura.* Santa Barbara, CA: Joshua Odell Editions.

Churchill, W. (1994). *Indians are us? Culture and genocide in native North America.* Monroe, ME: Common Courage Press.

Cobb, P., & Hodge, L. (2007). Culture, identity, and equity in the mathematics classroom. In N. S. Nasir & P. Cobb (Eds.), *Improving access to mathematics.* New York: Teachers College Press.

Darder, A. (2012). *Culture and power in the classroom.* New York: Routledge.

Delgado Bernal, D. (1998, Winter). Using Chicana feminist epistemology in educational research. *Harvard Educational Review, 68*(4), 555–582.

Diaz-Soto, L., Soon, C. C., Villarreal, E., & Campos, E. (2009). Xicana sacred space: A communal circle of compromiso for educational researchers. *Harvard Educational Review, 79*(4), 755–775.

Eglash, R. (2001). The race for cyberspace: Information technology in the Black Diaspora. *Science as Culture, 10*(3), 353–374.

Gallucci, C., Van Lare, M. D., Yoon, I. H., & Boatright, B. (2010). Instructional coaching: Building theory about the role and organizational support for professional learning. *American Educational Research Journal, 47*(4), 919–963.

Gandára, P., & Contreras, F. (2009). *The Latino education crisis: The consequences of failed social policies.* Cambridge, MA and London: Harvard University Press.

Goode, J. (2007). If you build teachers, will students come? The role of teachers in broadening computer science learning for urban youth. *Journal of Educational Computing Research, 36*(1), 65–88.

Grosfoguel, R. (2004). Race and ethnicity or racialized ethnicities?: Identities within global coloniality. *Ethnicities, 4*(3), 315–336.

Grosfoguel, R. (2008). *Transmodernity, border thinking, and global coloniality: Decolonizing political economy and postcolonial studies.* Berkeley: University of California.

Holland, D., & Lachiotte, W., Jr. (1998). *Identity and agency in cultural worlds.* Cambridge, MA: Harvard University Press.

Huanacuni Mamani, F. (2010). *Buen Vivir/ Vivir Bien Filosofía, políticas, estrate- gias y experiencias regionales andinas.* Lima, Peru: Coordinadora Andina de Organizaciones Indígenas—CAOI.

Johnston, A. (2007). Demythologizing or dehumanizing? A response to settlage and the ideals of open inquiry. *Journal of Science Teacher Education, 19*(1), 11–13.

Kahn, R. V. (2010). *Critical pedagogy, ecoliteracy, and planetary crisis: The eco- pedagogy movement.* New York: Peter Lang.

Karttunen, F. (1992). *An analytical dictionary of Nahuatl.* Norman, OK: University of Oklahoma Press.

Kirchhoff, P. (1943). *Mesoamerica: Sus límites geográficos, composición étnica y caracteres culturales.* México City: Escuela nacional de antropoligía e historia sociedad de alumnus.

Leban S., & McLaren P. (2010). Revolutionary critical pedagogy: The struggle against the oppression of neoliberalism—A conversation with Peter McLaren. In S. Macrine, P. McLaren & D. Hill (Eds.), *Revolutionizing pedagogy. Marxism and education.* New York: Palgrave Macmillan.

López-Austin, A. (1980). *Cuerpo humano e ideología. Las concepciones de los antiguos nahuas.* Mexico City: Universidad Nacional Autónoma de México, Instituto de Investigaciones Antropológicas.

Mander, J. (1992). *In the absence of the sacred: The failure of technology and the survival of the Indian Nations.* San Francisco, CA: Sierra Club Books.

Margolis, J., Estrella, R., & Goode, J. (2008). *Stuck in the shallow end: Education, race, and computing.* Cambridge, MA: MIT Press.

Martin, D. B. (2007). Mathematics learning and participation in the African American context: The co-construction of identity in two intersecting realms of experience. In N. S. Nasir & P. Cobb (Eds.), *Improving access to mathemat- ics.* New York and London: Teachers College Columbia University.

Martin, D. B. (2000). *Mathematics success and failure among African-American youth: The roles of sociohistorical context, community forces, school influence, and individual agency.* Mahwah, NJ: Lawrence Erlbaum.

Martin, D. B. (2009a). *Mathematics teaching, learning, and liberation in the lives of black children.* New York: Routledge.

Martin, D. B., & McGee, E. O. (2009b). Mathematics literacy for liberation: Reframing mathematics education for African American children. In B. Greer, S. Mukhophadhay, S. Nelson-Barber & A. Powell (Eds.), *Culturally responsive mathematics education* (pp. 207–238). New York: Routledge.

Martínez, E. (2009). *500 years of Chicana women's history, 500 años de la mujer chicana.* New Brunswick, NJ: Rutgers University Press.

McDermott, R., & Varenne, H. (1995). Culture as disability. *Anthropology & Education Quarterly, 26,* 324–348.

McLaren, P. (1988). Culture or canon? Critical pedagogy and the politics of lit- eracy. *Harvard Educational Review, 58*(2): 213–234.

McLaren, P. (2007). *Life in schools: An introduction to critical pedagogy in the foundations of education.* Boston: Pearson Education.

22   C. D. M. SANDOVAL

Milner, H. R. (2011). Culturally relevant pedagogy in a diverse urban classroom. *Urban Review, 43,* 66–89.

Moreno Sandoval, C. D. (2017). Exploring computer science for bi/multilingual learners: A case study using ancestral knowledge systems as border pedagogy in an East Los Angeles High School Classroom. In Ramirez, P. C., Faltis, C. J., and De Jong, E. J. (Eds.) *Learning from Emergent Bilingual Latinx Learners in K-12: Critical Teacher Education.* Routledge Press.

Moreno Sandoval, C. D., Mojica Lagunas, R., Montelongo, L., & Díaz, M. (2016). Ancestral knowledge systems: A conceptual framework for decolonizing research in social science. *AlterNative: An International Journal of Indigenous Peoples, 12*(1), 18–31.

Morrell, E. (2008). *Critical literacy and urban youth: Pedagogies of access, dissent, and liberation.* New York, NY: Routledge.

Omi, M., & Winant, H. (1974, September). *Racial formations in the United States.* London: Scientific American, Nature Publishing Group.

Omi, M., & Winant, H. (1994). *Racial formation in the United States: From the 1960s to the 1990s (critical social thought)* (2nd ed.). New York: Routledge.

Orfield, G., Losen, D., Wald, J., & Swanson, C. B. (2004). *Losing our future: How minority youth are being left behind by the graduation rate crisis.* Cambridge: The Civil Rights Project at Harvard University.

Paris, D. (2012). Culturally sustaining pedagogy: A needed change in stance, terminology, and practice. *Educational Researcher, 41*(93), 93–97.

Quijano, A. (1991). Colonialidad y Modernidad/Racionalidad. *Perú Indígena, 13*(29), 11–20. Lima, Peru: Instituto Indigenista Peruano.

Quijano, A. (1998). Colonialidad, Poder, Cultura y Conocimiento en América Latina. In *Anuario Mariateguiano, IX*(9), 113–122. Lima: Amauta.

Quijano, A. (2000). Coloniality of Power and Eurocentrism in Latin America. *International Sociology, 15*(2), 215–232.

Rennera, A., Brown, M., Stiens, G., & Burton, S. (2010). A reciprocal global education? Working towards a more humanizing pedagogy through critical literacy. *Intercultural Education, 21*(1), 41–54.

Sandoval, C. (2000). *Methodology of the oppressed.* Minneapolis: University of Minnesota Press.

Tyack, D. B. (1974). *The one best system: A history of American urban education.* Cambridge, MA: Harvard University Press.

Vaughan, D. (2002). Signals of interpretive work: The role of culture in a theory of practical action. In K. A. Cerulo (Ed.), *Culture in mind: Toward a sociology of culture and cognition* (pp. 28–54). New York: Routledge.

Viesca, C. (2003). Medicine across cultures: History and practice of medicine in non-western cultures. In H. Selin (Ed.), *Science across cultures: The history of non-western science book* (Vol. 3). Berlin: Springer.

Yosso, T. (2005). Whose culture has capital? A critical race theory discussion of community cultural wealth. *Race Ethnicity and Education, 8*(1), 69–91.

Yosso, T., & Solórzano, D. (2006, March). *Leaks in the Chicana and Chicano Educational Pipeline* (Latino Policy and Issues Brief, No. 13). UCLA Chicano Studies Research Center.

CHAPTER 2

Internalized Colonization, Unearthed: Student Activism for Social Change

In this chapter, we work toward **circling around the fire with a purpose**. This entails setting our intent within the context established in chapter one. We explore aspects of damage that is visited upon us when we engage in the false indulgence of blaming.

When we say "**cuando apuntamos el dedo, tres nos regresan a nosotros**" we mean that when we blame without ownership, we cannot grow. **Unearthing internalized colonization** helps us to tend the soil, and plant a **collective critical consciousness** that can carry us through our days. Drawing from our familias, we can bring it back home.

This empirical study is grounded within a non-Eurocentric epistemology that informs an Indigenous research paradigm (Lomas, 2007; Smith, 1999). The aim is to develop a learning ecology of positive identity formation and critical agency in a student-led organization, a high school computer science (CS) classroom, and in a larger schooling community. Since the influence of CS is inextricable from our ways of communicating, whether we are conducting warfare or creating sustainable environmental efforts, our aim is to challenge Eurocentric practices that speak only partially to our ancestral way of thinking and acting. Simultaneously, we seek to build a responsible, sustainable climate of critical producers of computing. We draw upon our general ancestral praxis of our families of this Western continent, as primarily informed by our elders and parents, principal knowledge-keepers-and-passers.

© The Author(s) 2019
C. D. M. Sandoval, *Ancestral Knowledge Meets Computer Science Education*, Postcolonial Studies in Education,
https://doi.org/10.1057/978-1-137-47520-6_2

We seek to (re)establish our positive collective identity so that our capacity to contribute academically within the institution can blossom while our dignity is held intact.

2.1   Ancestral Praxis: The Rooted (R)evolution[1] of Indigenous-Descent Identity Formation

The evolution of identities for people of specifically Mexican descent—and which can also apply more generally to groups historically vulnerable to colonialism—has been long construed by outsiders who sought to name us as the "other" during the first documented contact and who, through such construction, created the idea of race. The term "Indigenous" was first used by colonialists to describe "uncivilized" peoples. If we leap forward a few hundred years, we see the US Census' use of the term "non-White Hispanic." At the same time, "Latino" is used among progressive writers and within popular culture to identify people whose origin is in what they call "Latin America." The serious problem is that both *Hispanic* and *Latino* are terms that correspond to European history. The etymology of *Hispanic* is Latin: *Hispanic-us,* or *Hispania* in Spanish, meaning "pertaining to Spain or its people; esp. pertaining to ancient Spain" (*Oxford English Dictionary,* 2011). Using a term that acknowledges *only* European origins is profoundly demeaning to people whose ancestors are also native to this continent, not *just* Europe.

The term *Latino* is just as problematic as *Hispanic*. Like *Hispanic, Latino* is a term that points strictly to European origins. Of Spanish etymology, *Latino* is documented by the *Oxford English Dictionary* (2011) as early as 1880 as a Latino-Sabellian, an Italian stock. Today, *Latino* is used to refer to "a Latin American inhabitant of the United States" (*Oxford English Dictionary,* 2011). There are five instances in which this term is illustrated in the Europeans' prestigious dictionary. The first, in 1946, refers to "a university's program exchange of students with Latin America...where Latinos are usually looked on as sinister specimens of an inferior race." Later, in 1966, "...all Latinos, had encased themselves in cardboard boxes." In 1972, "America is meant to be a great melting pot... Its racial components—Blacks, Latinos, Chinese, Japanese...." In 1973, "a program was drawn by an action group composed of Blacks, Latinos, and Whites," and finally, in 1974, "Mr. Rhodes' home was broken into...by a man who appeared to be of Latino origin."

These examples are used to illustrate the definition of *Latino*, which emerges from a decidedly deficit view, even as it invokes European origins. Moreover, these terms impose a worldview that denies other inclusions that are just as valuable as the European standard. This chapter will dive deep into the topic of identity (r)EVOLution for people connected to ancestral knowledge by unearthing the historical depth and richness of the multiple confluences of culture as an academic practice on this continent.

Nonetheless, identity was not based on the idea of race in precolonial times. Instead, identity was based on the physical relationship to the land. Although this concept of identity does not delineate a utopian approach to social justice, it nonetheless connected us to the physical environment in novel ways. For example, the intentional shaping of Mayan heads was used to indicate status. So the question that lingered perhaps when one met a "foreigner" was not "What is your race?" but "Where is your family from?" It is only since colonial times that we have used the idea of race as a signifier to describe peoples based on, largely, phenotype and cultural differences. Today, urban centers are a reflection of migration patterns based on top-down forces that have imposed economic and political racial projects. Thus, urban schools are centers of potential cultural spaces where students and their families feel that they belong to a specific time and critically understand their socio-historical positions as a liberatory practice. The following two sections will describe the evolution of peoples of Anahuac descent. Following my discussion of identity formation under a coloniality of power and the process of decolonizing identities, I will position ancestral praxis in a cultural anthropological figured world (Holland & Lachiotte, 1998). This positioning will help in later analyses of Chapters 4–6 of identity and agency in cultural worlds. This will be followed by a literature review of works on countercultures to this European standard, as well as a discussion of the implications for learning in the CS classroom context.

2.2 Identity Formation Under the Coloniality of Power

In a society that is fixated on political labels for individuals who have been tagged by a series of numbers or a racial category, it becomes all too simple to categorize ourselves as boxed figurines with sharp edges and finite behaviors, like toys in a display. Race is a constructed phenomenon that does not exist in isolation. When we speak of the racial constructs that have emerged since the beginning of colonialism on the Western continent, is useful to explore the ways in which identity formation operates under a coloniality of power. Omi and Winant (1994) argued that racial constructs should be described as a process that is rooted in a complex history that suggests political activity and economic complexities. Racial formation, a theory that describes the obsession with our past and current perceptions of race, is useful to analyze racial projects across organizational levels of schooling practices. Racism is also a process that should be analyzed through a racial formation theory. Drawing on Gramsci's (1971) view of hegemony, Omi and Winant (1994) described the institutional processes of unequal dimensions of power that camouflage dominated groups' interests within the interests of power, thereby leading them to portray a superficial "interest" in non dominant groups. Racial projects (described in the next section) are clear examples of these institutional processes that reify dominant systems of power to reflect a Eurocentric, monolithic approach to learning. Racism is not a static concept, but rather a process in which racial projects are enacted in a situated and contested time and space.

In this study, *race* is defined as Omi and Winant (1994) described it, as an "unstable and 'decentered' complex of social meanings constantly being transformed by political struggle, that is, race is a concept which signifies and symbolizes social conflicts and interests by referring to different types of human bodies" (p. 55). Furthermore, in a racialized social structure, racial formation is a socio-historic process by which racial categories are created, inhabited, transformed, and destroyed. In their research, Omi and Winant (1994) set out to situate racial categories as they are represented within hegemony, the process through which society is organized and ruled based on Eurocentric notions of being, particularly when non dominant groups are forced to identify themselves with European concepts, thereby adopting Eurocentric notions of knowledge:

When you control a [wo]man's thinking you do not have to worry about his[her] actions. You do not have to tell him[her] not to stand here or go yonder. [S]He will find [her]his "proper place" and will stay in it. You do not need to send him[her] to the back door. [S]He will go without being told. In fact, if there is no back door, [s]he will cut one for [her]his special benefit. His[Her] education makes it necessary... History shows that it does not matter who is in power... those who have not learned to do for themselves and have to depend solely on others never obtain any more rights or privileges in the end than they did in the beginning. (Woodson, 1990 [1933])

Carter G. Woodson's (1990) observation on the colonization of the mind is still prevalent in today's schooling practices, since the standardization of curricula is privileged over the local knowledge of Indigenous peoples, which is a practice that relies upon Eurocentric epistemologies. Bonilla-Silva (2001) referred to the "internal colonialism perspective" (p. 28) proposed by a group of analysts who postulated that racism is structured by the colonial status of racial minorities in the United States. Although Bonilla-Silva did find some limitations in the internal colonialist perspective (upon which I will later expand in the limitations section of Chapter 3), he recognized the explicit value this perspective must describe a collective experience of a vulnerable group with the coloniality of power.

Situated within the matrix of various dynamics of power, urban schools reflect the state of a social system that is crisscrossed by axes of class, gender, race, age, nationality, region, politics, and religion (Apple, 1999). One of the greatest problems in urban schools today is the absence of the development of positive personal and academic identities among underrepresented minorities. Critical educational theory can revolutionize and inform the lens through which researchers, educators, and policymakers engage in educational inquiry, so that urban schooling participants—including students, educators, and parents—can alter current positivist practices of public schooling and claim a positive self-identity, which is invariably missing in the current climate of high-stakes accountability. By highlighting the complex ways in which knowledge is constructed and valued, critical educational theory, through the gaze of an Indigenous pedagogy, can inform a positive academic and personal identity formation. By recognizing the socio-economic construction of human knowledges, this can occur in the following ways: (1) it can challenge epistemologies in which positivist educational research values knowledge; (2) it can situate Indigenous peoples as decolonizing identities that promote a positive academic and personal sense of self and community; (3) it can create social transformation by embodying an Indigenous identity (worldview) as a critical self-reflexive practice to deconstruct positivist notions of being; and (4) it can advocate for community-based research as the center of educational inquiry in urban schools. Although this book carries implications that a multicultural populace may wish to critically self-reflect upon as it considers its own Indigenous heritage, I will focus on the experiences of the largest growing minority in the US: Xican@s whose ancestors are of Mexican Indigenous descent.

Critical educational theory is characterized by a Western European Marxist tradition that pushes to "liberate human beings from the circumstances that enslave them" (Horkheimer, 1982, p. 244). Generally, critical theory considers the shortcomings of current social reality, identifies the actors to change it, and provides both clear norms for criticism and achievable practical goals for social transformation. Informed by this theory, an Indigenous pedagogy is inclusive of sovereignty in the form of self-determination of humanity and ecology, explicit emancipatory agendas, and challenging notions of epistemic frames of Western theory, cultural, psychological, and ecological viability. For example, a sustainable approach para el vivir comunitario questions the ways in which hegemony-based decisions have stripped us away from humanist efforts to sustain the land and its resources. It is based on a historical hope in the understandings of our ancestors (Grande, 2004; Moreno Sandoval, Mojica Lagunas, Montelongo, & Díaz, 2016). Furthermore, an Indigenous pedagogy affirms that culture cannot be "added onto" or simply appended to existing school curricula because it leads to an "appreciation" of culture and language; instead, Indigenous knowledge must be placed in the center of discourse and action.

This book affirms the existence and knowledge of Indigenous peoples (Smith, 1999) of Mexican descent in urban schools. Utilizing Aronowitz and Giroux (1993) and Apple's (1999) "language of critique and possibility," I will argue for the inclusion of this identity as oppositional to urban schooling participants (Apple, 1999; Sandoval, 2000).

2.2.1   *Challenging Epistemologies of Human Knowledge*

Research is one of the ways in which the standardization of colonialism is both regulated and realized. It is regulated through the formal rules of individual scholarly disciplines and scientific paradigms, and the institutions that support them, including the state (Smith, 1999). Alternately to traditional practices, Cruz (2006) suggested that our production of knowledge begins in the bodies of our mothers and grandmothers, in the acknowledgment of the critical practices of women of color before us, for it is the experiences of women of color that inform the most disenfranchised spaces of political power (Comas-Díaz & Greene, 1994). As other scholars (Behar, 1996; Kincheloe & McLaren, 1994) have noted, a critical reflexivity through counter-stories (DeCuir & Dixson, 2004; Yosso, 2005) is essential if we are to dismantle the hegemonic epistemologies of human knowledge. But a critical consciousness is not enough to unravel the exclusionary traditions of neoliberalism. Individual and collective agency must follow a critical consciousness for the returning to ourselves with dignity. Thus, the (re)covery of an Indigenous knowledge system is crucial for the collective action of our state so it is paramount to critically distinguish between a Eurocentric standard of being and a decentered multiplicity of knowledge systems as we critically analyze the social, historical, political, and economic capital both operate under.

Eurocentric intellectuals habitually take the knowledge of Indigenous peoples and incorporate it into their own thinking, usually without attribution. In this process, non-Indigenous-identified people who appropriate culture often twist interpretations about Indigenous knowledge beyond recognition, says M. Annette Jaimes, "bending it to suit their own social, economic, and political objectives" (Churchill, 1994, p. 139). Thus, the need for critical methodologies *by* Indigenous peoples is essential to deconstruct traditional Eurocentric knowledge and to name Indigenous knowledge as inclusive understandings that are necessary to drive teaching and learning in urban schools. In the report *Between Two Worlds*, the Pew Hispanic Research Center (2009) confirmed the results of other scholars' thorough examinations (Suárez-Orozco & Suárez-Orozco, 1995), which have shown that students who identify as bicultural and biliterate tend to perform better in school and have more positive experiences (Darder, 2012).

2.3 Decolonizing Our Cultural/Academic Identities

"*Indigenous peoples*" is a term that emerged in the 1970s as an international attempt to bridge the struggles of the American Indian Movement and the Canadian Indian Brotherhood. In this book, this identity term is not limited to a static concept. Indeed, there are real differences among Indigenous peoples worldwide. I do not mean to suggest a pan-Indigenous view of the multiplicity of positions and experiences among Indigenous peoples. The term *Indigenous* has been defined as "born or produced naturally in a land or region" (*Oxford English Dictionary*, 2011). In fact, *Indigenous* comes from the Latin *indigena*, which means "native" to a region. Native peoples are communities or nations that have governed themselves according to their own worldviews. Indigenous people often carry creation stories that tell of an intricate ancestral knowledge that may evolve over time (Champagne & Abu-Saad, 2003). It is important to note that, while I provide a general description of Indigenous peoples here, self-identification is valued as a subversive act. It is also beyond the purview of this book to engage in the current obsession regarding identity politics and questions of authenticity that, although necessary, often obfuscate the socio-political and material conditions of Indigenous peoples. For Indigenous-descent peoples, identity politics has evolved with the interactions of governmental forces that impose rather than democratize.

German ethnologist Paul Kirchhoff (1943) identified common characteristics of pre-Columbian cultures (including Central and Southern Mexico, Guatemala, Belize, El Salvador, Western Honduras, Nicaragua, and Northwestern Costa Rica) that emerged over a 3500-year shared history. This array of cultures held similar or overlapping worldviews, which included but were not limited to calendrical and writing systems, ballgames, medicine and science, politics, and art. Today, Indigenous culture thrives as a shared practice that is overt and covert, sometimes even subconscious in the making. There is ample evidence available to trace the historicity of such current practices (Martínez-Cruz, 2011).

As a shared identity that unifies multiple cultures, a Mesoamerican worldview and identity could be a turning point for social transformation. While, of course, a worldview is "a [set of] fundamental beliefs, values, etc., determining or constituting a comprehensive outlook on the world; a perspective on life" (*Oxford English Dictionary*, 2011), I do not wish to specifically address the entire array of components that form a worldview—an impossible task. However, by drawing our attention to a shared history of Mesoamerica, we can cultivate—rather than deny—an Indigenous identity. Through such identification, we can learn to decode the imposed doctrines (Newcomb, 2008) and our native traditions. This informed position allows us to choose to adopt a worldview that is alterative and subversive with regards to our current situation, which seeks to assimilate or nationalize our conception of the self.

Cultivating a Mesoamerican identity for US residents of Mesoamerican descent is not a new concept. In Comas-Díaz's (2001) scholarship on the evolution of identity for "Hispanic/Latino" populations of the United States, she includes Xican@ as an identity that derives from the "Nahuatl pronunciation of Mexica or Mexicanos." The identification of Mexicas describes a group of Indigenous people commonly referred to as the Aztecs. In using *Xican@*, "which replaces the 'ch' in Chicano with the 'x,' the person affirms his or her Indigenous heritage" (Castillo, 1994, cited in Comas-Díaz, 2001, p. 118). The "x" stems from a Uto-Aztecan root that births Nahuatl. For us, the evolution of identity (Comas-Díaz, 2001) has developed through an awareness of the socio-political contexts of the time that we have occupied this land. The 1960s brought a newfound politicization to Mesoamerican descent people living in the United States. MEChA was formed and for the first time, we identified as Chicano on a large-scale consciousness:

> We, as Mechistas, see the process of Chicanismo as evolutionary. We recognize that no one is born politically Chicana or Chicano. Chicanismo results from a decision based on a political consciousness for our Raza, to dedicate oneself to building a Chicana/Chicano Nation. Chicanismo is a concept that integrates self-awareness with cultural identity, a necessary step in developing political consciousness...grounded in a philosophy, not a nationality. Chicanismo does not exclude anyone, rather it includes those who acknowledge and work toward the betterment of La Raza. (The Philosophy of Movimiento Estudiantil Chicano de Aztlan, 1969)

A Mesoamerican identity reclaims the shared cultural practices of a vast amount of time and space. If we were to create this common vision in the most densely populated areas of Mesoamerican heritage, a social transformation may develop, especially because in places like Los Angeles, through a network of movements, the subliminal visual discursive messages continue to spread rampantly. This network of movements materializes by the facilitation of social networking sites and the presence of Mesoamerican exhibits in various special commonplaces of social activity.[2] The social fabric that weaves a social dialectic of a Mesoamerican worldview centers the interconnectedness of all sentient beings. I defer to Mexica philosophy (currently, the most documented of the plethora of ethnic diversities of Mesoamerica), as described by

Jane Maffie (2005) to describe a specific worldview that is denied by Eurocentric standards of learning in public schools:

> The aim of cognition from the epistemological point of view is walking in balance upon the slippery earth, and epistemologically appropriate inquiry is that which promotes this aim. Nahua epistemology does not pursue goals such as truth for truth's sake, correct description, and accurate representation; nor is it motivated by the question "What is the (semantic) truth about reality?" Knotig (spatial)[3] is performative, creative, and participatory, not discursive, passive or theoretical. It is concrete, not abstract; a knowing how, not a knowing that. (Maffie, 2005)

Cowan's (2007) ethnographic study in central California analyzed a Mesoamerican visual discourse to explain the resistant practices of Mesoamerican youth using Boone's (1994) and Mignolo's (1995) notions that challenge the ethnocentric presumption that Mesoamerican cultures are less than Eurocentric standards and, therefore, should be dismissed in public schooling. Boone provided evidence that Mesoamerican communications, outside of a Eurocentric way of thinking of literacy, are what she calls *semasiográficos* of communication—"stemming from the Greek word, *semasia* that means 'significance' to indicate visual systems of communication where communication is directed and inside a structure of its own" (Boone, 1994, p. 15). Mignolo (1995) referred to this system of communication as "colonial semiotics" to include interactions that use signs to communicate as a form of literacy. Moreover, Cleary and Peacock (1998) have recognized differences in the thought processes of oral and civilizations Eurocentrically considered "literate" (i.e., having an alphabetic structure). Under such a definition, the Chinese would not be considered literate. People who stem from oral traditions, like Mesoamericans, contextualize our articulations of thought through the shared knowledge of the people who will be listening to us; communication is not divorced from a consideration of the reader as interrelated to the writer. Mesoamericans also have complex writing systems that can be universally interpreted by a multiethnic audience. *Mesoamerican's communication systems exist with and without writing, through oral and semiotic visual discourse.* What implications do visual discursive practices in urban schools have for social transformative possibilities here? Knowing that bicultural, acculturated youth do better in schools in general (Darder, 2012; Pew Hispanic Research Center, 2009), how can visual discursive practices bridge a bicultural and biliterate understanding for Mesoamerican-descent youth? Exploring this question is beyond the scope of this book, yet I pose it here as food for thought to continue our discourse around identity formation and agency in cultural worlds.

The tenets of an Indigenous pedagogy can address the concern of a nascent identity formation in urban schools. Validating Indigenous knowledge at the center of student inquiry will further advance higher education for Indigenous youth. During his years of teaching at a summer institute, Cowan (2007) observed the visual discourse of his students and noticed that, coupled with the historical knowledge they were learning from the center around Mesoamerican history, the students would use visual expressions that spoke volumes. In one case, one of his students, Alejandro, whom he later interviewed, illustrated a pyramid of books (including one entitled *Chicano history*) with a low-rider at the forefront and two revolutionary figures on opposite sides of the pyramid. Alejandro later explained that he considered his drawing as having the "mismo sentido espiritual de tu conexión a la vida que está muy, muy, muy profundamente arraigado, pasado de mano en mano de generación a generación."[4] Alejandro felt a deep connection to something larger than his own physical reality, to the memory of his ancestors that paved a path for him to walk. He was able to connect with the messages that have been passed on through oral tradition, visual discourse, and genetic memory. Alejandro reported his positive sense of self through his worldview as an intellect of higher learning and of Mesoamerican descent, representing the small percentage of the US Mesoamerican population that enrolls in university. This demonstrates his positive outlook regarding his identity as an *indígena* of Mesoamerican descent. The analysis of this book (in Chapter 5) will look at the ways in which Itzel, a high school junior of El Sereno, includes a visual discourse and dialogue of Mesoamerican cultural practices using computing for social change.

Other examples of unearthing the live Mesoamerican sense of self outside of a Eurocentric standard of being can be seen in a series of YouTube videos entitled "Mesoamerica in Aztlán" produced by Tocatzin and Fernando (Tocatzin, 2009–2010, January 6). The series illustrates ways in which Mesoamerica thrives in the life of urban areas today. For example, Tocatzin and Fernando showcase the El Sereno Community Garden as a hub of Mesoamerican visual discursive practices through arts. Another multimedia project, a collection of stories from people living in the United States, is entitled "Amoxtli san ce tojuan—We are one—Nosotros somos uno," produced by Patrisia Gonzáles and Roberto Rodríguez (2005). This is yet another example of living connections between our Indigenous present and our Indigenous past. Although it is impossible to perfectly place ourselves within the worldview of the ancients because the temporal commonplace has evolved, the connections that remain follow a thread of dialogue and action by Xican@s and our familias who work to peel away the layers of internalized colonization by planting our own foods, creating semiotic representations of the elements that we are connected to, that give us life. There is an increasing movement,[5] like the movement of a lively river rapidly tumbling toward the ocean, of US-residing Indigenous peoples of Mesoamerican descent who are becoming knowledgeable about and claiming their identity as a subversive act.

2.3.1   Creating Social Transformation by Embodying an Indigenous Identity and Worldview

Agreeing with Wallerstein (1991, 2003) and Grosfoguel (2008) ascertained that our social, collective agencies urgently need to be addressed so that we can create alternative worlds to our current exploitative, coercive system of disenfranchised societal systems in US territory. He explains that an increased bifurcation is emerging as the "European modern/colonial capitalist/patriarchal world-system" (Grosfoguel, 2004, p. 606) creates more tension. One possible scenario is that the twenty-first-century transnational capitalist elites could follow a strategy similar to the feudal aristocracy of the late fifteenth century and to keep their privileges intact, create a new historical system worse than the present one. The ruling class holds on to their power with tooth and nail. Another possibility is that subaltern groups around the globe, especially those within the metropolitan centers of capitalist world-system, can create a new and/or diverse historical system that challenges neo-liberal practices that continually erode our collective dignity. The significant growth in Mesoamerican-descent populations in the United States and our consequent political/cultural impact in the capitalist world-system today can lead to great strides in the social transformation of society. We can best contribute through an increased ancestral praxis to include the social imagination of our creative intellect within the arts, sciences, philosophies, ecological knowledge, health, nutrition, etc.—and through systematically questioning current uses of technological systems through a sustainable Mesoamerican worldview as developers of knowledge that is applicable to this social imagination.

Given their demographic growth and strategic location at the center of the US empire, the traditions, imaginaries, identities, and utopias that prevail within these populations in the twenty-first century will be a crucial factor in determining the future of the US empire and that of the capitalist world-system as a whole. By breaking down the walls of internalized racism (hooks, 1995) and affirming a non-European epistemic Indigenous worldview and identity, Mesoamericans could become a positive bridge between different groups and a healing anti-racist force within the country (Grosfoguel, 2004). This would be a bridge that leads by the example of "taking us to our own self-power" (Delgado Bernal et al., 2006) while dealing with our own colonialities through the critical self-reflexive practice (Anzaldúa, 1987) of decolonizing US imperialism. Guillermo Marin (2009) wholeheartedly agreed. In his conference presentation at the California Association for Bilingual Education in Long Beach on *Pedagogía Tolteca*,[6] he explained that Mexicans residing in the United States have the power to socially transform the United States and Mexico through the claiming and understanding of our identities as Indigenous peoples. We do this by cultivating identities not as a romantic return to some pure and idyllic identity, but rather as a recreation and reimagining of the present through cultivating a social imagination that decolonizes neoliberal practices of a "white supremacist capitalist patriarchy" (hooks, 1995).

2.3.2 Advocating for Indigenous Localized and Transcultural Community-Based Inquiry in Urban Schools

Beginning with students' own traditional knowledge—which is historically, culturally, and linguistically situated in their own bridging of immediate and ancient realities and applied to our current positions as urban residents—we have the power to transform society to regain our collective dignity as creative intellectual contributors to the fabric of our nations, beginning with young people. We are not unique in being Indigenous people. Ward Churchill (2003) states that everyone has an Indigenous ancestry, and it is the responsibility of each individual to position his/her identity in direct communication with his/her own traditional knowledge that is oppositional to the colonialist worldview of hierarchical domination:

The Indigenous peoples of the Americas can, have, and will continue to join hands with the Indigenous peoples of this land [Germany], just as we do with those of any other. We are reaching out to you by our very act of being here, and of saying what we are saying to you. We have faith in you, a faith that you will be able to rejoin the family of humanity as peoples interacting respectfully and harmoniously- on the basis of your own ancestral ways- with the traditions of all other peoples. We are now expressing a faith in you that you perhaps lack in yourselves. But, and make no mistake about this, we cannot and will not join hands with those who default on this responsibility [of cultivating an ancestral worldview/identity], who instead insist upon wielding an imagined right to stand as part of Europe's synthetic and predatory tradition, the tradition of colonization, genocide, racism, and ecocide. (Churchill, 2003, pp. 243–244)

Ward Churchill (2003) ended with a call to all peoples of the world to reconnect with their ancestral pasts as a subversive act that may lead to an alternative system, a return to protecting human integrity and humane ecology. Mesoamericans in the United States can paddle the canoe on that river strongly and quickly, teaching and learning toward a positive critical self-image as contributors to knowledge and as actors during a critical turning point in society's values. Through this practice, we will be joining other Indigenous relations of this Western Hemisphere and leading by example. Urban schools are the center of opportunity for this inquiry to develop and extend from and into the surrounding community, so that social transformation can emerge.

2.4   The Figured World of Ancestral Praxis as a Framework for Understanding Identity and Agency

Developed as a cultural anthropological framework, figured worlds are stable and "shared realm[s] of interpretation in which a particular set of characters and actors are recognized, significance is assigned to certain acts, and particular outcomes are valued over others" (Holland & Lachiotte, 1998, p. 52). It is helpful to think about these figured worlds as processes, rather than as static lived experiences or labels. Participants in these worlds voluntarily enter or are recruited for participation. It is important to note that figured worlds do not exist statically across time and space; rather, they are locally and temporally instantiated and determined by the positions of individuals who are socially organized and reproduced. These socially constructed worlds are maintained through interactions, which divide/relate participants, and are populated by familiar social types. In addition, figured worlds provide a framework in which to study collective action by:

> spreading our senses of self across many different fields of activity, but also by giving the landscape of human voice and tone. Cultural worlds are populated by familiar social types and even identifiable persons, not simply differentiated by some abstract division of labor. (Holland & Lachiotte, 1998, p. 41)

Ancestral praxis as a "figured world" provides a means to conceptualize historical subjectivities, consciousness, and individual and collective agency formation in practice. Figured worlds also provide practical terms for making sense of the complexities of human agency, which can be understood as

> the realized capacity of people to act upon their world and not only to know about or give personal or intersubjective significance to it. That capacity is the power of people to act purposively and reflectively, in more or less complex interrelationships with one another, to reiterate and remake the world in which we live, in circumstances where we may consider different courses of action possible and desirable, though not necessarily from the same point of view. (Inden, 1990, p. 23, cited in Holland & Lachiotte, 1998, p. 42)

In this book, I look at human agents as we make sense of the world by drawing on our ancestral praxis to form our identities as a counterculture to the dominant norm in formal and informal spaces. This identity formation feeds our sense of acting in the world for communal wellness as we, for example, challenge CS practices and socially produce responsible uses of technology. Inden (1990) continued to share his thoughts on human agency: "People do not act only as agents. They also have the capacity to act as 'instruments' of other agents, and to be 'patients,' to be the recipients of the acts of others" (p. 23, cited in Holland & Lachiotte, 1998, p. 42).

Sfard and Prusak (2005) pushed us to think more deeply about people's lived realities and the fact that our perceptions are contextualized by our living experiences. As opposed to personality, character, or nature, identity is thought of as constantly created and recreated in interactions between people (Roth, 2004 as cited in Bauman, 1996; Sfard & Prusak, 2005) as active agents who play decisive roles in determining the dynamics of social life and in shaping individual activities (p. 15).

In particular, they described identity as helpful in dealing with issues of power, as well as in addressing the question of how "collective discourses shape personal worlds and how individual voices combine into the voice of a community" (p. 15). To use identity as an operational framework of analysis of human conduct, the authors noted that we must take on the challenge of thinking about identities as stories. The identities we gain within figured worlds are specifically historical developments, grown through continued participation in the positions defined by the social organization of these worlds' activity systems.

The stories we use to make sense of the world, individually and collectively, encode the figuring of these worlds that organize knowledge and guide inferences. These cultural models guide actions and self-understandings to reinterpret historical events. Stories of identity, "as cultural mediating devices" (Holland & Lachiotte, 1998, p. 88), are tools for reinterpreting the past and putting the self into the socially constructed world. Identity talk helps us make sense of the world in relation to others, makes us able to cope with new situations in terms of our past experiences, and gives us tools for the future.

2.4.1   What Is Ancestral Praxis?

Ancestral praxis refers to the socio-historical processes of Indigenous people throughout the world. At its core, ancestral praxis involves a marriage as a *process* between generational theory and practice. Ancestral praxis is not a static concept so it cannot be captured in a way that is easily encapsulated by a label, rather a process that involves interactions with intercultural groups and power relations. This study focuses on the ancestral praxis of the majority in the El Sereno schooling community. This knowledge is drawn upon as an epistemic practice aimed at recycling knowledge within our current societal context. This means that our ancestral praxis systems are fluid because they change over time and context. So what "worked" 3500 years ago may not necessarily apply to today's context. Praxis changes over time as our world evolves. The purpose of this work is to underline ancestral praxis systems of our community cultural wealth, as prefaced by Xicana feminist epistemological work (Delgado Bernal et al., 2006). This is a way to engage in the world by recognizing the impact of an outside dominant Eurocentric structure imposed upon us through current-day colonialist practices in and out of formal learning spaces. The embedded forms of ancestral praxis are demonstrated by a developing collective consciousness of families within communities. These practices are passed down from one generation to the next through cultural ways of knowing, such as storytelling, language use, body language, food cultivation and preparation, ceremonial practices, and behavior. Within the practice of our current ancestral ways, there is a strong critical consciousness that is shared multi-generationally through culturally specific ways of teaching and learning. Through these practices, there is subtle and sometimes explicit socio-historical telling of colonization, resistance, segregation, value systems, and sanctity. These memories help us "survive in everyday life by providing an understanding of certain situations and explanations about why things happen under certain conditions" (Delgado Bernal et al., 2006, p. 30). Sara Lawrence-Lightfoot (1994) agreed. She affirmed that "ancestral wisdom" is shared generationally, and called it "a powerful piece of our legacy" that is "healthy" and "necessary for survival," and that "maintain[s] and transmit[s] an entire culture, a worldview complete with proven strategies for survival" (cited in Delgado Bernal, 1998, p. 558). Because communal[7] wellness (as opposed to disconnected and individualized activities) is at the center of a Mesoamerican ancestral worldview, prioritizing the overall emotional, physical, spiritual, and intellectual/creative health of the *collective*. Moreover, because the survival of the environment is just as important as our own well-being, we draw upon the knowledge systems of agriculturalist societies (vs. warrior-like, empire-like societies) (Sapolsky, 2005; Textor, 1967) that have a visceral understanding of the natural cycles of the environment. After all, ancient societies can be traced to specific locations and times, and can recount lifestyles that are directly connected to their environments. Later, in Chapter 5, I will describe how a CS classroom can incorporate the cultural ancestry of underrepresented adolescents in an urban context through ancestral computing.

The following eight tenets attempt to describe a basic guiding philosophy of ancestral praxis from the perspective of the El Sereno schooling participants that attended a workshop on "What is Indigenous?" sponsored by Lomas High School MEChA that sparked the creation of this guiding philosophy. These points are to be used in dialogue and action, according to the specific time and space in which each schooling community is contextualized. They are not to be taken literally or as dogma, but rather as roadmaps that may resonate cross-culturally. Ancestral praxis points of dialogue and action include:

1. Explicit understanding is expressed regarding the interconnectedness and deep respect for all sentient beings, including plant nations, two-legged, four-legged, and winged nations, water, fire, air, wind, elements, rock nation, and the star nation. For example, there is a common phrase that is invoked in circles that work toward embodying ancestral praxis: "hunab kú"[8] (Martínez Paredez, 1973, cited in Hoopes, 2009), which loosely translates as "you are my other me."
2. An underlined communal, family spirit pervades social interactions, even when we agree to disagree and strive to (re)develop collective wisdom.
3. A special focus on and recognition of the development of cultural intuition (Delgado Bernal et al., 2006) prioritizes family interactions with all generations alike. Special attention is paid to the preservation of connections to root culture through food preparation, language, body language, and maintaining connections to family/land in place of origin.
4. There is a practice of developing a critical consciousness through reflection, paying special attention to differentiating between colonizing and decolonizing practices specific to a socio-historical context (sometimes by reading anthropological scholarship).
5. Maintain a holistic view of body, mind, spirit, and psyche, and the interrelations between them. This also means developing emotional intelligence and personal development to "know thyself" while critically acknowledging current obsessions with our self-image.
6. There is a strong consideration of time and space (Deloria & Wildcat, 2001) as links to today's context. For example, we cannot be certain about the thoughts of the ancient ones when they began the process of domesticating corn on this continent, yet we can conclude that the generations that continued the practice of domestication were building collective efforts *over time* to ensure that corn would grow rampantly to feed the people. What collective force will we build upon today for the future generations of tomorrow? By the same token, we know that the ancient ones

identified with the relationship to the land (Berdan et al., 2008), rather than strictly phenotypic characteristics, so having a strong connection to the environment in which we live in is another piece of knowledge.

7. El darnos a respetar means that we value our positionalities so much that we would assertively care for our contributions to our families and our communities. This self-respect includes a respect for others, including past generations. For example, considering that in this neoliberalist time, a disregard and isolation of teens and elders is normative. Multigenerational family ties and participation in schools are essential for educational excellence. It is all too often painful to consider this option in our pueblos today for the coloniality of power has ripped families apart (through restrictive immigration and language policies, the epistemicide of nondominant populations in schooling practices, etc.) and it may strike a sensitive chord to consider reconciling with our biological family members where a critical approach to emotional intelligence, respect, and acceptance can go a long way.

8. We seek the cultivation of collective agency or force. For example, if we look at the *Huehuetlatolli*, Book VI of the Florentine Codex, we find a reference to some advice that a father gave to his daughter. In it, the nobles mention "our force" or fuerza, as one of the pleasures in life. How else could we build long-standing structures, if not as a collective force?

Finally, I share the following poem that was written and shared during the end of a twenty-day count celebration, Xochiilhuitl, on our Mesoamerican calendar in the spring of 2011, in which we celebrated the blooming of flowers. The poem shares another perspective on honoring ancestral praxis today.

IPaMPa ZaN CE iHIYOTL ToYOLiZ
īpampa zan cē ihīyōtl toyōliz
IPaMPa ZaN QUeTZaLTEMiCTLi ToYOLiZ
īpampa zan qūetzaltēmictli toyōliz
TLA CeNTLi ToCoNCUACAN
tlā centli toconcūācān
TLA XOCoLATL ToCoNICAN
tlā xōcolātl toconīcān

IPaMPa ZaN aCHiC TiToTLaNEHUICoH iN TLALTiCPaC
īpampa zan achic titotlanēhūīcoh in tlālticpac
TiQUiMMaHUiZOCAN
tiqūimmahūizōcān
ToCiHHUAN ToCOLHUAN ToNANHUAN ToTAHHUAN
tocihhūān tocōlhūān tonānhūān totāhhūān
TiQUiNTLaZoHTLaCAN
tiqūintlazohtlacān
ToCiHUAHUAN ToPoHHUAN
tocihūāhūān topohhūān
iN MaCHiYOTL TiQUiMMaNaLiCAN
in machiyōtl tiqūimmanalicān
ToCOCoNEHUAN ToPIPiLHUAN
tocōconēhūān topīpilhūān

iN IC PaHPAQUiCAN
in īc pahpāqūicān
ToTLaZoHCAiLaMaTZITZiNHUAN
totlazohcāilamatzītzinhūān
iN IC PaHPAQUiCAN
in īc pahpāqūicān
ToTLaZoHCAHUeHHUENTZITZiNHUAN
totlazohcāhūehhūēntzītzinhūān
TLA ToNCUICaCAN
tla toncūīcacān
TLA ToNTiHTOTICAN
tlā tontihtōtīcān

iN MoCHi TLeH TLoQUeH NAHUaQUeH

TiQUiMiTTaCAN
iN MoCHi TLeH IPaL NeMoHUaNi TiQUiMiTTaCAN
iN MoCHi TLeH MoYOCoYaNi TiQUiMiTTaCAN
iN MoCHi TLeH OMeTeOTL TiQUiMiTTaCAN

iPaMPa NiCAN TiCaTeH
iPaMPa NiCAN TiHCaQUeH
iN IC aYIC TiPoLiHUiZQUeH
iN IC aYIC TiLCAHUaLOZQUeH

ToXOCHiUH ToCoNCHaYAHUaCAN
ToCHALCHiUH ToCoNCHaYAHUaCAN

ToTONaL ToCoMPOHUaCAN
ToZAZANiL ToCoMPOHUaCAN
ToTLaHTOL ToCoNEHUaCAN
ToPAN ToCoNEHUaCAN

Porque nuestra vida es solo un suspiro
Porque nuestra vida es solo un hermoso sueño
Sembremos maíz
Comamos amaranto
Bebamos chocolate

Porque solo un breve instante venimos a prestarnos unos a otros en
la Tierra
Honremos nuestras abuelas, nuestros abuelos, nuestras madres,
nuestros padres
Amemos nuestras mujeres, nuestros compañeros
Tendamos un ejemplo para
Nuestros niños

Para que nuestras amadas ancianas sean alegres
Para que nuestros amados ancianos sean alegres
Cantemos
Bailemos

En todas las cosas veamos a Tloqueh Nahuaqueh
En todas las cosas veamos a Ipalnemohua
En todas las cosas veamos a Moyocoyani
En todas las cosas veamos a Ometeotl

Por eso somos aquí
Por eso estamos aquí
Para que nunca nos perdamos
Para que nunca seamos olvidados
Esparsamos nuestras flores
Esparsamos nuestros jades
Contemos nuestros días
Contemos nuestras historias
Elevemos nuestra palabra
Elevemos nuestro estandarte

Porque nuestra vida es solo un suspiro

Porque nuestra vida es solo un hermoso sueño
Sembremos maíz
Comamos amaranto
Bebamos chocolate

Porque solo un breve instante venimos a prestarnos unos a otros en
la Tierra
Honremos nuestras abuelas, nuestros abuelos, nuestras madres,
nuestros padres
Amemos nuestras mujeres, nuestros compañeros
Tendamos un ejemplo para
Nuestros niños

Para que nuestras amadas ancianas sean alegres
Para que nuestros amados ancianos sean alegres
Cantemos
Bailemos

En todas las cosas veamos a Tloqueh Nahuaqueh
En todas las cosas veamos a Ipalnemohua
En todas las cosas veamos a Moyocoyani
En todas las cosas veamos a Ometeotl

Por eso somos aquí
Por eso estamos aquí
Para que nunca nos perdamos
Para que nunca seamos olvidados
Esparsamos nuestras flores
Esparsamos nuestros jades
Contemos nuestros días
Contemos nuestras historias
Elevemos nuestra palabra
Elevemos nuestro estandarte

—Cuezalin y Huitzilmazatzin
Xochimecayahualli
19 de marzo del 2011
Ceremonia de Xochiilhuitl

Because our life is just a breath
Because our life is just a beautiful dream

Let us plant corn
Let us eat amaranth
Let us drink chocolate

Because only briefly we come to lend ourselves to each other on
Earth
Let us honor
Our grandmothers, our grandfathers, our mothers, our fathers
Let us love our womben and men companions
Let us lay an example for our children
So that our beloved elder womben be happy
So that our beloved elder men be happy
Let us sing
Let us dance

In all things let us see Tloque Nahuaqueh
In all things let us see Ipalnemohua
In all things let us see Moyocoyani
In all things let us see Ometeotl

That is why we are here
That is why we are here
So that we will never perish
So that we will never be forgotten

Let us scatter our flowers
Let us scatter our jades
Let us count our days
Let us tell our stories
Let us raise our voice
Let us raise our banner

—Cuezalin and Huitzilmazatzin
Xochimecayahualli
March 19, 2011
Xochiilhuitl Celebration of the Flower

This poem tells about how we may (re)imagine our lives today, while considering the level of resistance to the colonial forces that we interact with on a daily basis, particularly within our own internalized colonial practices. A special focus is placed on our ancestral foodways, song and dance, and multigenerational relations, within a deep understanding to the interdependence with our environment, nuestra Madrecita Tierrecita.

2.5   Ancestral Praxis in a Computer Science Classroom

For the Indigenous peoples of the planet, Mother Earth is life itself. We human beings are an integral part of the nature and meaning and we always practiced a lot of respect for her. For thousands of years we have lived with nature in constant balance with it and within it. Today, we feel the devastating effects of neoliberal transnational capitalist system rapidly destroying our planet. (Morales, 2009)

For some it is difficult to fathom the juxtaposition of the terms computing and Indigenous pedagogy. The *Oxford English Dictionary* (2000) defines computing as "the action or an instance of calculating or counting" and gives the first documented occurrence of the word appearing in 1629 as "Neuerthelesse the number of the Lacedæmonians may be attained by computing thus." The second definition refers to the uses of an electronic computer. Today, the use of electronic computers is an all-too-often unquestioned consumerist approach to living, not quite considering the physical and social sustainability of its existence. For example, do we ever consider the material that is used to build these digital technologies? Where does the material originate? How is it processed? Where does it go after it becomes obsolete? For considerations of these and other issues, I propose we turn to ancestral computing as a process that engages issues of social and physical sustainability, and at large, broader participation in computing.

Pohua in Classical Nahuatl is defined as "to count; to read; take note of in a census; to relate; to measure." Mesoamerican descent peoples have one of the most intricate calendrical systems in recorded history. This book reveals the act of computing as an ancestral practice that has existed in ancient civilizations for millennia. It is with this understanding that Mesoamerican descent peoples can see ourselves as computational thinkers that are confronted with an evolved approach to measuring the world through digital technology. The popular approach to digital computing today was initiated by human mathematicians like Katherine Johnson who was "a computer" at Langley Research Center in the early computing days.

Today, electronic computing, or technological systems, are both socially constructed and society shaping (Hughes, 1987). Dominant modern computing has largely been informed by a globalized "white supremacist, capitalist patriarchy" (hooks, 2000, p. 159) that is divorced from Indigenous epistemologies. More notably, cyberspace, a popular sector of computer science, began as a child of military expediency, and its "technological superiority provided justification for the mythology of genetic differences in intelligence, the means of domination, and the colonial" (Eglash, 2001, p. 356). In 1983, the Defense Advance Research Projects Agency, a division of the U.S. Department of Defense, issued a document that speared a proposal of a thousand-fold increase in computing power over five years, the "Strategic Computing Plan" to develop a new generation of military applications for computers (Mander, 1992). As such, computer science, as a branch of science, is a field that has pedagogically been void of diverse perspectives of the world (Buckingham, 2008; Harding, 1998; Rosser, 1995).

In this chapter section, I draw out the complexities of a changing world localized in urban schools as I explore the question, "How might an Indigenous pedagogy inform a computer science curriculum?" After laying out a basic description of computer science and Indigenous pedagogy as positivist, separate worlds, I will focus on three areas that may provide insight into ways in which urban schooling students can most benefit when an Indigenous pedagogy informs computer science curriculum. First, historicizing and building upon coding and computational thinking as part of students' Indigenous knowledge systems promotes a positive ethnic and academic identity (Martin, 2000). Second, centering Indigenous ways of knowing with computer science situates students' realities and connects them to their communities and ecologies. Driven through self-inquiry and reflexive practice, students find solutions to everyday problems in a way that also leads them to seek social transformation. Third, students connect to various cultural environments through interdisciplinary discourses.

2.5.1   Computer Science and Indigenous Pedagogy, a Description of Historically Separate Worlds

While computer science is defined as "the branch of knowledge concerned with the construction, programming and operation and use of computers" (*Oxford English Dictionary*, 2000) the field's "impact on society" (Deek et al., 2003, p. 6) is the specific focus for curricular development in this book. Although there may be significant differences between the terms *computer science, digital media, technology, Internet* and *cyberspace*, I will use the terms synonymously as I discuss their common characteristics. The underlying commonality of these digitally technical processes are all descriptors of creations that are based in or rely on "computer science." Computer science is a discipline that serves as a tool that has applicable properties for a range of disciplines from the sciences to the arts. CS is a field that is transforming the ways we communicate with the world in our personal, professional, academic, and political lives, yet an undiversified "exclusive band of our population is learning the skills and techniques imparted by computer science" (Margolis et al., 2008, p. 4). Within computer science's

> urban and First World bent; its masculine and white nature; its predisposition toward the English language; its isolating nature (community is achieved only with a very individualized and lonely interaction with a machine); the information overload and triviality of images; and the Internet's inherent visual bias. (Brook & Boal, 1995, cited in Froehling 1997, p. 293)

its development demonstrates narrow components of the neocolonialist practices and characteristics of computer science.

Naturally, resistance builds where there is tension between hierarchical dynamics of power (Apple, 1999; Darder, 2012). Jerry Mander (1992) provided a series of claims with his publications on advocacy against technology, advocating for its abolishment for the survival of Indian Nations. He furthered his argument by demonstrating how harmful technology has been to Indigenous peoples, who traditionally have been left out of the developments of computer science. In this book, I will add complexity to Mander's argument within the context of Indigenous peoples in present-day urban schooling practices. I will offer a discussion around the reciprocal relationship that urban Indigenous peoples might have with computing as mutual informants and call this relationship between Indigenous knowledges and modern day digital technology, ancestral computing. I use the term *ancestral* as synonymous to *Indigenous* because it links a generational connection to a lineage of people, however, I use both terms *ancestral* and *computing* to discuss a temporal relationship between people and tools.

"Indigenous" as an identity is not limited to a static concept. In this book, it is not understood as an all-encompassing notion that spans the multiplicity of positions and experiences among Indigenous peoples. The term *Indigenous* is defined as "born or produced naturally in a land or region" (*Oxford English Dictionary*, 2000). In fact, Indigenous comes from the Latin word—*indigena*—which means "native." And "Native peoples are communities or nations that have...governed themselves according to their own rules, and often have religious or creation stories that provide specific forms of [language], government, culture and territory" (Champagne & Abu-Saad, 2003). The current Mexica Movement calls this identity, *nican tlaca*, loosely translated to "we are here."

Although Indigenous peoples use technology in their everyday lives, the recent phenomenon of computer science lacks a critical perspective. It lives in an isolated world of zeroes and ones that purport to advance national competition with other nations. This book proposes an inter-relationship between an Indigenous pedagogy and computer science curriculum. An Indigenous pedagogy is centered in the ancient ways of teaching and learning. At its heart, an Indigenous pedagogy purports to be a guide to placing students' Indigenous knowledge at the center, thus acknowledging that students' knowledge is valued outside the standard dynamics of power that essentialize "other" types of knowing and/or push them to the periphery.

Mander's position against technology offers us insight into the complicated ecologies of "modernization." It is true that technological advancements for the sake of "modernizing" society have harmed the earth in a variety of ways—from their toxic production of material use and abusive waste sites to the ways in which they have excluded groups of people from participating as civically engaged participants. Nonetheless, it is more complex than this. In the hands of a privileged few, computer science contributions have augmented the globalization process, which has pulled individuals away from their immediate environments. In other words, technological advancements have given us the tools to obtain information in seconds from across the globe, and, thus, are moving us away from localized forms of knowledge. At the same time, computer science is a powerful tool that has transformed a society, and the urban city in particular. It is used for a variety of purposes, and teenagers are using technology at higher rates than ever before. A study conducted by the Pew Research Center showed that some 75% of 12–17-year-olds own mobile phones, up from the 45% in 2004 who used text messaging as a main form of communication, with 50% sending 50 or more text messages a day (Lenhart, 2010). It would be quite drastic to advocate for the abolishment of technology for young people.

Churchill (1994) focused our attention on the fact that Mander, although pushing for Indigenous rights, chose to include very few Indigenous peoples themselves in his analysis of technological dangers to Indian Nations and the environment. Although Churchill (1994) agreed that Mander brought up some important arguments against technology, Churchill contested the fact that he only cited or quotes three Indigenous people as "props, orchestrated by and large to accompany Mander's own 'universal' themes" (Churchill, 1994, p. 150). The list of contemporary native "leaders and philosophers" Mander mentioned is a gross underrepresentation. He included three Indigenous scholars as contributors to knowledge, while actually silencing their collective voices. This, Churchill contended, perpetuates disregard for Indigenous intellectualism. We must find a common ground in which we can use and create socially responsible technologies that will place Indigenous issues at the center of teaching and learning.

2.6   WHEN INDIGENOUS WAYS OF TEACHING AND LEARNING CHALLENGE TRADITIONAL COMPUTER SCIENCE TEACHING AND LEARNING

Ron Eglash (2001) acknowledged the blatant exclusion of racial groups from computer science production. However, instead of rejecting technology, Eglash proposed that researchers look into and validate the rich computational thinking that lives in the Indigenous practices of students' historical knowledge systems. He asked us to consider the following question: "How do utterances of scientists [...] literally move and shape worlds, channel flows of institutional funding, and exert enormous influence in shaping the meaning of life?" (p. 354). The binary code appears to have a distinct African origin (Eglash, 1999). Coined by Leibnitz around 1670, the binary code system traces its roots back to the alchemists' divination practice of geomancy (Eglash, 2001), which is not of European origins. Eglash continued to contest the dynamics of power by explaining that the traditional purview of technophilia often supposes that minority groups wait for information technology for salvation, rather than examining the unacknowledged traditions of computation and coding from Indigenous peoples.

Another way in which Indigenous groups have utilized technologies for social transformation was when the North American Free Trade Agreement (NAFTA) entered into force on the first day of January 1994. That day, the Ejército Zapatista de la Liberación Nacional (EZLN, or the Zapatistas) occupied seven towns in the Mexican state of Chiapas (Froehling, 1997). Their unexpected presence directed the focus from a globalized policy to the resistance of Indigenous peoples. Their demands created a network of supporters and disseminated information worldwide on a massive scale. In this case, a group of Indigenous peoples used web design and video production to spread the news of their subversive acts. Through this medium, the Zapatistas used computer science for a specific purpose that challenged the neocolonialist practices that forced them to push back in opposition.

Similarly, *Ventana A Mi Comunidad*,[9] a project of the Secretaría de Educación Pública (SEP), produced by the Intercultural and Bilingual Coordination Office of Mexico, is a series of short videos narrated by members of communities that illustrate their Indigenous practices of language, medicine, games, song, and other cultural elements. The videos include elders' and children's knowledge as it is pertinent to their roles in the community. The creators of the series of videos provide a narration that teaches the audience about Indigenous knowledge systems as practiced today through animation, video, and music. In this case, Indigenous communities share their teachings and learning ways of knowing. This is an example of how a community is using computer science to preserve its culture and reinforce a positive self-image that incorporates knowledge that has been preserved subversively for a very long time. In this way, Indigenous communities become the producers of knowledge.

What would these types of practices look like in the classroom setting? By using advanced technology and programming, students can begin to deconstruct their worlds through inquiry. Building on a set of problem-solving skills, students could identify an issue that they wish to research in their communities. For example, students could focus on access to healthy foods to prevent higher diabetes and high blood pressure rates in their families. After developing their research questions, they could use mobile phones to collect images of examples of foods available in their neighborhoods: produce, fast foods, grandmothers' fruit trees, etc., and categorize them accordingly. They could also record oral histories of their grandparents and create a living document online with their stories in order to preserve knowledge. After analyzing their own data, they could statistically and qualitatively narrate a powerful story. Their story could advocate for awareness within their communities about, for example, decolonizing diets using ancestral and native foods as a cure for the onslaught of illnesses facing their communities. This is but one example that could be used to integrate bicultural understanding of self-knowledge and Western knowledge.

In their report on their use of information technology, the Tomas Rivera Policy Institute issued a report entitled *Latinos and Information Technology: The Promise and the Challenge* (Tornatzky, Macias, & Jones, 2002) that aimed to increase engagement of technology by increasing diversity rather than addressing epistemological shifts in the ways technology is produced. Sponsored by the IBM Corporation, the report's goal is to focus national attention on how nondominant populations can more "successfully engage and prosper by the expansion of Information Technology into their every aspect of modern life" (Tornatzky et al., 2002, p. i). This would be achieved through higher educational proficiencies and adaptation of "their cultural norms and behaviors to an entrepreneurial, fast-moving and global approach to business and life" (Tornatzky et al., 2002, p. i). It called for initiatives that would make digital technology more "culturally relevant" to underrepresented populations in the field. But it is not enough to call for greater access to these learning tools. We must also engage in CS in the very ways that CS has been denied to specific cultural groups. The context of CS production is imperative for innovation and subversive action. Operating with the preexisting cultural capital that exists within local communities is key for students to claim ownership of their learning and application, so that the community at large will support their efforts to maintain a relationship to schooling practices.

Returning to the term *Indigenous,* native to the land, the focus of computer science through an Indigenous pedagogy presupposes the use of the collective historical experiences of the community as the context for all learning in the school. As Deloria and Wildcat (2001) stated, Indigenous peoples who historically and culturally connect to places can and do draw on power located in these places. When educators are asked to incorporate students' background knowledge, despite standardized curricula, it becomes nearly impossible to *centralize* (rather than merely incorporate when appropriate) learning within students' locations and histories. Like Paulo Freire (1970), who learned to read his world through literacy practices, students, too, must own their learning experiences through their socio-historical locations. Educating Indigenous peoples means that educators, as people who openly admit to being learners who value and practice continual critical self-reflection, must become participant observers in the community in a way that communicates genuine care (Valenzuela, 1999) and concern.

2.6.1   Ancestral Praxis + Critical Computer Science Education = Social Transformation

Ron Eglash (2001) broadened "the category of 'information technology' to show how traditions of coding and computation from Indigenous African practices [...] have supported, resisted, and fused with the cybernetic histories of the West" (p. 353). He concludes that access to such information could potentially reconstruct identity, social positions, and access to power for underrepresented communities in computer science.

Faye (2001) described his experiences teaching Native science to students of Western science. In this case, we discuss the opposite of our previous examples, in that Native science is at the center of knowledge for students who are non-Indigenous. Similar to the Pew Study (2009) on bicultural students living between two worlds, Faye (2001) found that teaching bilingually was the best approach. He would succeed in demonstrating the efficacy of Native science while validating Western science. In the meantime, he would include connections between both languages, thereby advancing the pluralism of knowledge systems in the classroom setting. Similarly, the Pew Study (2009) found that youth who identified as bicultural and bilingual on a national survey that measured identity were more likely to succeed in school. Self-identified Indigenous computer science learners have the ability to transform society.

2.7   Socio-Cultural Historical Learning Theory as Agency Toward Communal Wellness

The public discourse and educational policy around measuring success in schooling focuses on "objective" measures like test scores and educational attainment. This approach to defining learning in public schools often looks at cultural differences from a deficit viewpoint, like a stereotype threat (Steele, 1997), which overlooks the dire need to shift public discourse to *start with and also include* the historical and sociological underpinnings through the critical analysis of power and social structures in which learning contexts take place.

Sfard and Prusak (2005) used individual and collective storytelling as analytic tools to investigate learning as a culturally shaped activity: "The object of learning may be the craft of cooking, the art of appearing in media, or the skill of solving mathematical problems, depending on what counts as critical to one's identity" (p. 19). Thus, how students see themselves as learners greatly influences their action toward learning. Nasir and Hand (2006), along with other scholars, argued that

> identity is a critical mediator of learning and that how students view themselves as learners can greatly influence how they participate in educational activities and settings and, conversely, how teachers and institutions participate can come to greatly influence how students view themselves as learners...learning is not only about taking on new knowledge structures, but it is about personal transformation—about becoming. (p. 467)

Some students may adopt an identity that is oppositional to the institutional achievement of "success." For example, Wortham (2007) illustrated this with the case of Maurice in a 9th-grade US English and history class. Maurice tried to "maintain an identity both as a student who makes valuable contributions in class and as an adolescent male respected by his peers" (Wortham, 2007, p. 741). Sometimes these identities conflicted when there was tension at the heart of Maurice's social identity in the classroom, and when he was forced to choose one side of himself over the other. In this case, Wortham concluded that learning changes one's position within one's community.

Danny Martin (2009) contended that mathematics education for nondominant groups contextualizes learning *not* as a desire to close the so-called achievement gap, which only leads to nondominant groups achieving a European model of success. Instead, Martin shone light on a critical approach of mathematics learning that positively demonstrates the mathematical abilities of nondominant cultures so that underrepresented students can see themselves as *doers* of mathematics while maintaining a positive cultural identity. He calls for mathematics learning to (1) challenge hegemony; (2) establish perceptions of positive ethnic and academic identities; and (3) be emancipatory, with students becoming agents of their own learning and communal development.

NOTES

1. (r)EVOLution is used in this study as a play on letters to describe a word. Like ancient writing systems of the Maya, for example, letters and sounds were compounded together to form words, visually as well as phonetically. There is an algorithm to the composure of words in ancient writing systems of the Mesoamerica. Here, I use (r)EVOLution to describe revolution, evolution, and LOVE all in one. I have seen it in anonymous public art and decided to include it here in my academic voice, which includes genetic memory of the past, using current underpinnings.

2. Here, the reference to spatial commonplaces refers to a focus of a Critical Narrative Inquiry (other foci consider temporal and social commonplaces to tell a story). The Aztec Pantheon at the Getty Villa (2010) displayed the Florentine Codex to the West for the first time since it was sent to Europe during the sixteenth century. A collection of twelve encyclopedic books, the Florentine Codex is a "divine collection that was made to be kept alive" (Magaloni Kerpel, 2012) through the use of chemical makeup of color, technique, image and power of the text. In addition, the Olmecs inhabited LACMA for months, beginning in September 2010, and in 2012 they displayed *The children of the plumed serpent: The legacy of Quetzalcoatl* as an examination of art and material objects of late pre-Columbian times. These exhibits were made possible by collaboration with the Instituto Nacional de Arqueología e Historia (INAH), along with other organizations, a transcultural exchange that pushed for a strong presence of Mesoamerican artifacts in the US. Here are some reflexive questions about the reliquias that grace us with their presencia: What is inspired from the presence of these reliquias? What message remains for us as we apply ancestral worldviews to today's context?

3. *Tlamatiliztli* "knowledge" is the nominalization of the verb-*tlamati* "to be knowledgable" (Karttunen, 1982).

4. The English translation would be: "it's that same spiritual feeling of your connection to life, and it's very, very, very profoundly rooted, passed on from one hand to the next, from generation to generation." All translations by author unless otherwise noted.

5. The use of social networking sites provides a means to remain connected with individuals with similar interests. As such, social networks are facilitated to create and sustain cultural activities that reinforce an alterative approach to living within a neoliberalist state that forges a Europeanization of being.

6. "Toltec pedagogy" presentation given at the *California Association for Bilingual Education* in Long Beach, CA, entitled "35 years promoting promising practices for English learners: Releasing multilingual dreams today, creating new worlds tomorrow," February 25–28, 2009.

7. With my use of *communal*, I include our interrelated connections to the natural world. We see the natural cycles of the elements interact with one another as they destroy and reproduce life. The movement of the electromagnetic field is respected and considered when dialoguing around issues that move our social interactions.

8. "In his book *Hunab Kú: Síntesis del pensamiento filosófico maya*, Martínez Paredez (1973, pp. 26–27) writes: '... trajo como consecuencia admirable el que el pensador maya llegase a la genial conclusión de que EL TU es mi OTRO YO, con la expresión IN LAK'ECH, ERES MI OTRO YO... mis aspiraciones son las de que algún día esta lección de nuestros antepasados mayas, sirva para conciliar al hombre con el hombre, que la humanidad reflexione y sepa decir como el filósofo maya a su prójimo: ¡IN LAK'ECH—ERES MI OTRO YO!" (Hoopes, 2009).

9. *Ventana A Mi Comunidad* is a series of YouTube videos that are produced by the Secretaría de Educación Pública in Mexico. "Serie de videos Ventana a mi Comunidad. Una producción de Videoservicios Profesionales SA de CV para la Coordinación General de Educación Intercultural y Bilingüe de la Secretaría de Educación Pública, México."

REFERENCES

Anzaldúa, G. (1987). *Borderlands: The New Mestiza = La Frontera*. San Francisco: Spinsters/Aunt Lute.

Apple, M. W. (1999). *Official knowledge: Democratic education in a conservative Age*. New York: Routledge.

Aronowitz, S., & Giroux, H. A. (1993). *Education still under siege*. Westport, CT: Bergin and Garvey.

Bauman, Z. (1996). From pilgrim to tourist—Or a short history of identity. In S. Hall & P. du Gay (Eds.), *Questions of cultural identity* (pp. 18–36). London: Sage.

Behar, R. (1996). *The vulnerable observer: Anthropology that breaks your heart*. Boston, MA: Beacon Press.

Berdan, F. F., Chance, J. K., Sandstrom, A. R., Stark, B., Taggart, J., & Umberger, E. (2008). *Ethnic identity in Nahua Mesoamerica: The view from archaeology, art history, ethnohistory, and contemporary ethnography*. Salt Lake City: University of Utah Press.

Bonilla-Silva, E. (2001). *White supremacy and racism in the post-civil rights era, Lynne*. Boulder, CO: Rienner.

Boone, E. H. (1994). Aztec pictorial histories: Records without words. In E. H. Boone & W. D. Mignolo (Eds.), *Writing without words: Alternative literacies in Mesoamerica and the Andes* (pp. 50–76). Durham and London: Duke University Press.

Buckingham, D. (2008). *Youth, identity, and digital media*. Cambridge: MIT Press.

Champagne, D., & Abu-Saad, I. (Eds.). (2003). *The future of Indigenous people: Strategies for survival and development*. Los Angeles, CA: UCLA American Indian Studies Center.

Churchill, W. (1994). *Indians are us? Culture and genocide in native North America*. Monroe, ME: Common Courage Press.

Churchill, W. (2003). *Acts of rebellion: The ward churchill reader* (pp. 243–244). London: Psychology Press.

Cleary, L., & Peacock, T. (1998). *Collected wisdom: American Indian education*. Boston: Allyn & Bacon.

Comas-Díaz, L. (2001). *Hispanics, Latinos, or Americanos:* The evolution of identity. *Cultural Diversity and Ethnic Minority Psychology, 7*(2), 115–120.

Comas-Díaz, L., & Greene, B. (1994). *Women of color: Integrating ethnic and gender identities in psychotherapy*. New York: The Guilford Press.

Cowan, P. M. (2007). ¡Adelante! Conectándose al pasado, anhelando el futuro a través del discurso visual latino. *Revista Mexicana de Investigación Educativa, 12*(34), 951–986.

Cruz, C. (2006). Toward an epistemology of a brown body. *International Journal of Qualitative Studies in Education, 14*(5), 657–669.

Cuezalin and Huitzilmazatzin. (2011, March 19); Xochimecayahualli. Xochiilhuitl Celebration of the flower.

Darder, A. (2012). *Culture and power in the classroom*. New York: Routledge.

DeCuir, J., & Dixson, A. (2004). *"So when it comes out, they aren't that surprised that it is there"*: Using critical race theory as a tool of analysis of race and racism in education. *Educational Researcher, 33*(5), 26–31.

Deek, F., Jones, J., McCowan, D., Stephenson, C., & Verno, A. (2003). *A model curriculum for K-12 computer science: Final report of the ACM K12 Task Force Curriculum Committee*. New York, NY: Computer Science Teaching Association.

Delgado Bernal, D. (1998, Winter). Using Chicana feminist epistemology in educational research. *Harvard Educational Review, 68*(4), 555–582.

Delgado Bernal D., Alejandra Elenes, C., Godinez, F. E., & Villenas, S. (Eds.). (2006). *Chicana/Latina education in everyday life: Feminista perspectives on pedagogy and epistemology*. Albany: State University of New York Press.

Deloria, V., & Wildcat, D. (2001). *Power and place: Indian education in America*. Golden, CO: American Indian Graduate Center, Fulcrum Resources.

Eglash, R. (1999). *African fractals: Modern computing and indigenous design*. New Brunswick, NJ: Rutgers University Press.

Eglash, R. (2001). The race for cyberspace: Information technology in the black diaspora. *Science as Culture, 10*(3), 353–374.

Faye, J. (2001). Subverting the captor's language: Teaching Native science to students of Western science. *American Indian Quarterly, 25*(2), 270–273.

Freire, P. (1970). *Pedagogy of the oppressed.* New York, NY: Herder and Herder.

Froehling, O. (1997). The cyberspace "war of ink and internet" in Chiapas Mexico. *American Geographical Society, 87*(2), 291–307.

Gonzáles, P., & Rodríguez, R. (2005). *Amoxtli san ce tojuan: We are one—nosotros somos uno.* San Fernando, CA: Xicano Records and Film. Wallerstein (1991, 2003).

Gramsci, A. (1971). *Selections from the Prison Notebooks of Antonio Gramsci.* New York: International Publishers.

Grande, S. (2004). *Red pedagogy: Native American social and political thought.* New York: Rowman & Littlefield.

Grosfoguel, R. (2004). Race and ethnicity or racialized ethnicities?: Identities within global coloniality. *Ethnicities, 4*(3), 315–336.

Grosfoguel, R. (2008). Latin@s and the decolonization of the US empire in the 21st century. *Social Science Information, 47*(4), 605–622.

Harding, S. G. (1998). *Is science multicultural? Postcolonialisms, feminisms, and epistemologies.* Bloomington, IN: Indiana University Press.

Holland, D., & Lachiotte, W., Jr. (1998). *Identity and agency in cultural worlds.* Cambridge, MA: Harvard University Press.

hooks, b. (1995). *Killing rage: Ending racism* (1st ed.). New York, NY: H. Holt and Co.

hooks, b. (2000). *Where we stand: Class matters.* New York, NY: Routledge.

Hoopes, J. B. (2009). *Acceptance and interpersonal functioning: Testing mindfulness models of empathy.* Austin, TX: The University of Texas at Austin.

Horkheimer, M. (1982). *Critical theory.* New York: Seabury Press.

Hughes, T. P. (1987). The evolution of large technological systems. In W. Bijker, T. Hughes, & T. Pinch (Eds.), *The social construction of technological systems.* Cambridge: Massachusetts Institute of Technology.

Inden, R. (1990). *Imagining India.* Oxford: Blackwell.

Karttunen, F. (1982). Nahua history. In G. Collier et al. (Eds.), *Inca and Aztec states, 1400–1800: Anthropology and history (studies in anthropology)* (pp. 395–417). New York: Academic Press.

Kincheloe, J. L., & McLaren, P. L. (1994). Rethinking critical theory and qualitative research. In N. K. Denzin & Y. S. Lincoln (Eds.), *Handbook of qualitative research* (pp. 138–157). Thousand Oaks, CA: Sage.

Lawrence-Lightfoot, S. (1994). *I've known rivers: Lives of loss and liberation.* Reading, MA: Addison-Wesley.

Lenhart, A. (2010). *Teens, cell phones and texting.* Washington, DC: Pew Research Center Publications.

Lomas, J. (2007). The in-between world of knowledge brokering. *British Medical Journal, 334,* 129–132.

Maffie, J. (2005). *Internet encyclopedia of philosophy.* Aztec Philosophy. Available at https://www.iep.utm.edu/aztec/.

Magaloni Kerpel, D. (2012). *Los colores del nuevo mundo: Artistas, materiales y la creación del códice florentino.* Mexico City: Universidad Nacional Autónoma de México.

Mander, J. (1992). *In the absence of the sacred: The failure of technology and the survival of the Indian Nations.* San Francisco, CA: Sierra Club Books.

Margolis, J., Estrella, R., & Goode, J. (2008). *Stuck in the shallow end: Education, race, and computing.* Cambridge, MA: MIT Press.

Marin, G. (2009, February 27). *Pedagogía Tolteca.* Paper presented at the California Association for Bilingual Education Annual Conference, Long Beach, CA.

Martin, D. B. (2000). *Mathematics success and failure among African-American youth: The roles of sociohistorical context, community forces, school influence, and individual agency.* Mahwah, NJ: Lawrence Erlbaum.

Martin, D. B. (2009). *Mathematics teaching, learning, and liberation in the lives of black children.* New York, NY: Routledge.

Martinez-Cruz, P. (2011). *Women and knowledge in Mesoamerica: From East L.A. to Anahuac.* Tuscon, AZ: University of Arizona Press.

Martínez Paredez, D. (1973). *Hunab Kú: Síntesis del pensamiento filosófico maya.* Mexico City: Editorial Orión.

Mignolo, W. D. (1995). *The darker side of the renaissance: Literacy, territoriality, and colonization.* Ann Arbor: University of Michigan Press.

Morales, E. (2009, May 29). *Letter of Evo Morales to the continental indigenous summit.* Paper presented at the Continental Summit of Indigenous Peoples, Abya Yala Puno, Peru, La Paz.

Moreno Sandoval, C. D., Mojica Lagunas, R., Montelongo, L., & Díaz, M. (2016). Ancestral knowledge systems: A conceptual framework for decolonizing research in social science. *AlterNative: An International Journal of Indigenous Peoples, 12*(1), 18–31.

Nasir, N. I. S., & Hand, V. (2006). Exploring sociocultural perspectives on race, culture, and learning. *American Educational Research Association, 76*(4), 449–475.

Newcomb, S. (2008). *Pagans in the promised land: Decoding the doctrine of Christian discovery.* Golden, CO: Fulcrum Publishing.

Omi, M., & Winant, H. (1994). *Racial formation in the United States: From the 1960s to the 1990s (critical social thought)* (2nd ed.). New York: Routledge.

Oxford English Dictionary. (2000). Oxford University Press.

Oxford English Dictionary. (2011). Oxford: Oxford University Press.

Pew Hispanic Research Center. (2009). *Between two worlds: How young Latinos come of age in America.* Available at http://www.pewhispanic.org/2009/12/11/between-two-worlds-how-young-latinos-come-of-age-in-america/. Accessed May 8, 2011.

Rosser, S. V. (1995). *Teaching the majority: Breaking the gender barrier in science, mathematics, and engineering.* New York, NY: Teachers College Press.

Roth, W. M. (2004). Identity as dialectic: Re/making self in urban school. *Mind, Culture, and Activity, 11*(1), 48–69.

Sandoval, C. (2000). *Methodology of the oppressed.* Minneapolis: University of Minnesota Press.

Sapolsky, R. (2005). The influence of social hierarchy on primate health. *Science, 308*(5722), 648–652.

Sfard, A., & Prusak, A. (2005). Telling identities: In search of an analytic tool for investigating learning as a culturally shaped activity. *Educational Researcher, 34*(4), 14–22.

Smith, L. T. (1999). *Decolonizing methodologies: Research and indigenous peoples.* London: Zed Books.

Steele, C. (1997). A threat in the air: How stereotypes shape intellectual identity and performance. *American Psychologist, 52*(6), 613–629.

Suárez-Orozco, C., & Suárez-Orozco, M. M. (1995). *Transformations: Immigration, family life, and achievement motivation among Latino adolescents.* Redwood City, CA: Stanford University Press.

Textor, R. B. (1967). *A cross-cultural summary.* New Haven, CT: HRAF Press.

The Philosophy of Movimiento Estudiantil Chicano de Aztlan. (1969). Available at http://www.cwu.edu/~mecha/documents/phyiosophy.pdf.

Tornatzky, L. G., Macias, E. E., & Jones, S. (2002). *Latinos and information technology: The promise and the challenge.* Claremont, CA: The Tomás Rivera Policy Institute.

Valenzuela, A. (1999). *Subtractive schooling: U.S. Mexican youth and the politics of caring.* Albany, NY: State University of New York Press.

Ventana A Mi Comunidad is a series of YouTube videos that are produced by the Secretaría de Educación Pública in Mexico. "Serie de videos Ventana a mi Comunidad. Una producción de Videoservicios Profesionales SA de CV para la Coordinación General de Educación Intercultural y Bilingüe de la Secretaría de Educación Pública, México".

Woodson, C. G. (1990 [1933]). *The mis-education of the Negro.* Trenton, NJ: Africa World Press.

Wortham, S. (2007). The interdependence of social identification and learning. *American Educational Research Journal, 41*(3), 715–750.

Yosso, T. (2005). Whose culture has capital? A critical race theory discussion of community cultural wealth. *Race Ethnicity and Education, 8*(1), 69–91.

CHAPTER 3

Planting Seeds of Hope: Teacher Collaboration to Support Student Inquiry

This **study's methodology** highlights the differences between heart-centered, careful planning while taking into account ancestral lifeways, home stressors, isolation, and other factors. Furthermore, this work challenges the perspectives of "rigid" Eurocentric methods of study, which does not often encourage real engagement with self, home, community, and the world.

Interdisciplinary visions and commitments must be kept in mind, to ensure the gap between students employing ancestral praxis (AP) intersect with nonparticipating students in a meaningful and sensible set of outcomes. One method designed into this study hinges upon the participating computer science (CS) teacher should be of European descent— that is to say, specifically and intentionally not indigenous— and to perform deep critical inquiry into the relationship between this teacher and three Chicano activists with which he worked closely.

Inspecting these relationships, biases, agreements, and mechanisms help us design evolutionary methods to tend our seeds of hope.

The motivation for this research is to explore identity formation and agency in sites of AP and CS learning toward communal wellness (including educational excellence) by the collective agency of schooling participants in an urban high school context. The initial probing of this study was activated by a group of students who sought to promote cultural awareness and connections to the community on campus. This study illustrates how student inquiry can co-construct organizational influence and

© The Author(s) 2019
C. D. M. Sandoval, *Ancestral Knowledge Meets Computer Science Education*, Postcolonial Studies in Education,
https://doi.org/10.1057/978-1-137-47520-6_3

agency at the meso-classroom-level and macro-neighborhood scale. At its core, this book is a counter-narrative to the dominant structures of colonialism that inextricably shape a distorted image of ourselves as non-dominant peoples. For this reason, I draw upon an indigenous research paradigm (Lomas, 2007; Smith, 1999) that is not divorced from the AP of the key participants in this study. This work maintains accountability to relationships that shape our reality: ideas and exchanges with all our relations, including the environment and institutional spaces like schools. For researchers to be accountable to all of our relationships, we must make careful choices in our selection of topics, methods of data collection, forms of analysis, and the way in which we share information (Lomas, 2007).

This chapter will detail the methodology that has informed the process toward building a learning foundation of AP and CS in spaces at three organizational levels in schools: (1) a campus-wide student-led organization at an urban high school; (2) a single CS classroom, and (3) a multicampus extended schooling community situated within one of Los Angeles's 277 neighborhoods. These organizational levels are not to be taken as static components. They influence each other in fluid ways as they interact with one another. As part of a Narrative Inquiry and counter-narrative, I describe my positionality as a researcher using an auto-ethnographic account that follows my journey as a native, resident, and scholar-activist in the schooling community of focus. Finally, I describe the limitations of this book.

The goal of this study is to uncover the critical components for building a learning foundation of positive cultural and academic identities for Mexican-descent populations in sites of CS learning. I draw upon historical AP systems (Moreno Sandoval, Mojica Lagunas, Montelongo, & Díaz, 2016) in an urban CS high school classroom to improve our understanding of teaching and learning of nondominant populations in CS, a field with only miniscule representation of these populations. I also draw upon Tara Yosso's (2005) notion of community cultural wealth to restructure the traditional teaching and learning of CS in an urban context that is devoid of indigenous methodological approaches. Specifically, I detail the AP practices of a community's cultural wealth as they are carried out in a CS classroom, in a school, and in neighborhood contexts so that we "remember something ancient [to] imagine something new" (Chrystos, 1983, p. 57) for communal wellness as a labor of love.

3.1   RESEARCH DESIGN: A DESIGN EXPERIMENT OF NARRATIVE INQUIRY IN THE FIGURED WORLD OF ANCESTRAL PRAXIS

3.1.1   A Design Experiment

I have taken many methodological cues from Ann Brown's (1992) research as a design scientist who attempted to engineer innovative educational environments while simultaneously conducting experimental studies of those innovations as a systemic whole. The nature of the program that I am working with is inextricably connected to various aspects of teaching and learning, both formal and informal. In order to survey a holistic approach to innovative research methodologies, it is useful to think of this research as a design experiment in bridging complex systems. The approach that I offer to this research and the unique standpoint from which I originate informs the practice of a comprehensive program that is growing nationally, Exploring Computer Science (ECS), funded by the National Science Foundation.

Because I glean techniques from both European and non-European methodologies, a design experiment understanding of this research can lend itself to traditions from both sides of the world. Through this study, I seek to develop a theoretical model of learning and instruction that is rooted in a firm empirical base. For example, when I document student learning, a design experiment is useful for documenting learning as understanding. This is done through stories that the students and teacher share about their experiences with AP and CS. We now turn to the discussion of the use of Narrative Inquiry in this book.

3.1.2   A Critical Narrative Inquiry

In order to broaden the study of Mexican-descent peoples in CS education, I utilize storytelling as a familiar way of knowledge (re)production (Delgado Bernal, 1998; Delgado Bernal, Alejandra Elenes, Godinez, & Villenas, 2006; Solorzano & Yosso, 2002). Narrative inquiry captures and leverages participants' interpretive and inventive processes of thinking and acting, particularly in areas of identity and agency. After all, "humans are storytelling organisms who, individually and socially, lead storied lives" (Connelly & Clandinin, 1990, p. 2). A story is "a portal through which a person enters the world and by which his or her experience of the world is interpreted and made personally meaningful. Viewed this way, narrative is the phenomenon studied in inquiry" (Connelly & Clandinin, 2006, p. 477). Sfard and Prusak (2005) agreed. In their work on identity formation in mathematics education, they argued that individuals are "significant narrators" (p. 18) of their own life experiences and that as humans, we make sense of the world around us through the expression and collective meaning of that evolving, non-static narrative. The study of narrative, then, becomes the study of the ways humans experience the world. This means that AP is a construction and reconstruction of personal and social stories that name patterns of inquiry for this study. Because of the possibility for the development of a voice that stems from our historicities, Narrative Inquiry allows for an alignment with critical theory (Connelly & Clandinin, 1990), feminist studies (Clandinin & Connelly, 1988), and participatory action research methods (Camarrota & Fine, 2008; Lewin, 1946; Morrell, 2008). In addition, a Narrative Inquiry approach allows me to simultaneously situate identity formation and agency processes in temporal, social, and spatial commonplaces across three organizational levels of study.[1]

Connelly and Clandinin (2006) suggested that one must consider seven issues when conducting Narrative Inquiry. These are useful as illustration here because they informed the development of this study. As narrative inquirers, we go through the process of: (1) imagining a lifespace; (2) living and telling as starting points for collecting field texts; (3) defining and balancing the commonplaces; (4) investment of the self in the inquiry; (5) developing researcher–participant relationships; (6) considering the duration of study; and (7) composing relationship ethics and Narrative Inquiry. This study explores the stories of schooling participants as they interact with identity formation and agency in the cultural worlds (Holland, & Lachiotte, 1998) of AP and CS learning para el vivir comunitario. As a scholar-activist and resident of the schooling community of study, Narrative Inquiry as a methodology allows for my positionality to interact with the area of inquiry using my own cultural intuition (Delgado Bernal et al., 2006).

Lomas High School is the only comprehensive public high school of El Sereno. It is perched atop the rolling hills of El Sereno, overlooking the large metropolis to which it belongs, Downtown Los Angeles. Toward the south, the city skyline is a daily reminder that we belong to the second-largest urban area in the United States. And even though we are nestled atop the hills of El Sereno in one of the largest concrete jungles in the country, Lomas High School is near the Ascot Hills, a 140-acre state park of green space that is home to a variety of wildlife, including coyotes, jackrabbits, red tail hawks, snakes, hummingbirds, and owls.

Lomas is a public high school that had recently moved into small learning community contiguous spaces. It had also recently changed from a six-period schedule to a four-by-four eight-period block schedule. Most of the Lomas High School students come from two communities that have a strong Mesoamerican presence. Their residents, businesses, and public art are lively examples of rich cultural expression. Lomas High School's student population is 93.5% Mesoamerican, 3.5% Asian, and 1.2% African American (DataQuest, 2010). The majority of the student population lives in low-income households, and 72% of students are on free or reduced lunch, while the school's unemployment rate rose to 15.3% from 6.7% in 2007 (Rogers, Bertrand, Freelon, & Fanelli, 2011). Earlier (in Chapter 1), I cited the national graduation rate crisis of Mesoamerican students: only 68% graduate after four years (Orfield et al., 2004). The College Opportunity Ratio is a three-number figure that reports how many students graduate after four years and how many students complete the requirements to enter the CSU/UC system of higher education. Lomas High School fares lower than the national average of graduating Mesoamericans (100:42:21). Only 42 of 100 students entering 9th grade in 2005 graduated in 2009, and only half of these students were eligible for consideration in the CSU/UC system. I chose to work at Lomas High School because it is the schooling community that is home to my paternal family. When I joined the ECS team at UCLA as a graduate student, I made sure to select Lomas High School as one of my sites of inquiry. I will go deeper into my family background in a subsequent section on the macro-context of this study.

As part of each of my visits to Lomas High School, I offered my informal saludos[4] to the Parent Center, which sits conveniently close to the entrance of the school, with an open-door policy. As my visits became frequent and even predictable, the coordinator of the Parent Center prepared a form for me to go through the process of becoming a formal member. I was granted a "parent group" identification card that provided me staff-like standing in terms of access to the campus. I did not need to wear the "visitor" badge when I entered campus. The parent group is another campus-wide organization that is connected to other campuses in the neighborhood. I was initially introduced to Don[5] Guillermo, self-identified P'urhépecha[6] of Michoacan, Mexico, by another teacher at Lomas High School. Don Guillermo teaches parent classes at multiple school sites, including three in El Sereno. His classes are entitled "Acción Positiva,"[7] and they use AP as leverage for communal wellness.

To explore these spaces, which are related to my central question, I begin with the narratives of students and parents at the school level to discuss the following questions: What is ancestral computing? What affordances/constraints does ancestral computing have toward decolonizing identities? How may campus-wide student-led initiatives carry over into the institutional classroom space as a tool for learning? How may AP and computing systems leverage agency of schooling participants toward communal wellness and educational excellence?

3.6   MESO-LEVEL: COMPUTER SCIENCE CLASSROOM AT LOMAS HIGH SCHOOL

Several factors played into my decision to include the CS classroom space as the mesocosm of this study as a possibility for situated action across organizational levels (Vaughan, 2002). It is worthwhile to study the classroom in urban schools so that we can work toward building a foundation of learning that is institutionalized in its inception. During the initial stages of my grounded thinking around this work, I noticed an ongoing thread of conversations that parents and elders had about young people today. They expressed concern that young people were not learning how to work the land as they themselves had when they were of a similar age. Instead, youngsters were glued to their television screens, playing video games, or hooked on social networking sites. Worse yet, parents and elders were concerned that the "machine" would dictate the ways in which society developed itself and replace human interactions. Jerry Mander (1992) believed that digital technology must be completely eradicated from our society if Indigenous Nations were to survive. He viewed technology as a representation of the absence of the sacred and its failure to incorporate a sustainable environment for all peoples. As I learn, participate in, and observe the field of CS in today's society, I, too, am deeply troubled by the manner in which decisions are made about the creation of this powerful tool. However, this tool has the ability to create as well as to destroy. It is disturbing that the backgrounds of those who create this technology do not reflect the backgrounds of those who consume or, more importantly, are affected by it.

The technologies that currently exist are created from the perspective of a select few, mostly white males who hold points of view that are not necessarily representative of most the consumer population. For this reason, it is paramount for our populations to understand what we are dealing with, from the perspective of a *producer*, rather than merely as a consumer. ECS a project funded by the National Science Foundation that is dedicated to democratizing CS. The ECS mission is to broaden participation in computing in the Los Angeles area and beyond.

This study looks at the ECS classroom as a nexus for inquiry toward developing a learning foundation of AP. The curriculum is divided into six units, including: (1) Human–Computer Interaction, (2) Problem-Solving, (3) Web Design, (4) Introduction to Programming (using Scratch),[8] (5) Data Collection and Analysis, and (6) Robotics (using LEGO NXT Mindstorms).

The teacher in this study, Mr. Allan Adams, has been a leader in the implementation of ECS at Lomas High School. He also teaches business entrepreneurship and chemistry. Allan lives about forty miles from El Sereno, and he also plays in a band that performs for events and concerts. He can pretty much play any instrument without the music in front of him. He is very good at organizing time for his students. I chose this classroom because I have maintained a positive working relationship with Allan throughout our collective participation and implementation of a two-year UCLA Center X[9] grant entitled, "DietSens: Mobilizing ancestral memory, advanced technology and student inquiry/engagement for health in a community and high school of El Sereno[10]." We have planned, taught, and reflected together over the course of three years. We have realized that, while we come from quite distinct backgrounds and have many differences in our teaching styles, we have worked together well, with a lot of mutual learning. I chose

Allan as the educator participant in my study because it is important to learn from implementing a culturally relevant pedagogy with a teacher who may not have a background in critical race theory or whose background does not reflect the cultural background of his students. This context is useful to inform the majority of the teaching profession in this country, which increasingly does not reflect the cultural backgrounds of students (Howard, 2003).

3.7   RESEARCH QUESTIONS

The three organizational clusters of sub-questions, shown in Table 3.1, helped guide my data collection, analysis, and discussion.

Table 3.1   Research questions

Foundational research question		
How may Mesoamerican academic cultural practices provide a foundation for a positive learning ecology of cultural academic identities in three organizational levels of a public high school, especially in spaces that have been historically segregated, like CS education?		
Lomas High School MEChA	CS Classroom	El Sereno Neighborhood Schooling Community
Micro-level	Meso-level	Macro-level
Informal	Formal	Informal
Sub-Questions:		
• How may student inquiry co-influence positive collective identities and agencies for communal wellness, including educational excellence?	• How do participants make sense of and act upon AP and CS intersections over time?	• How may student-led initiatives and classroom practices inform a neighborhood-wide schooling movement towards general wellness, including educational excellence?

3.8   MACRO CONTEXT: THE SCHOOLING COMMUNITY OF EL SERENO

For at least 180 days, teens, preschoolers, parents, educators, administrators, and staff come together to become part of the learning community at Lomas High School in El Sereno. However, not all of these participants live in El Sereno; some come from neighboring barrios such as City Terrace, Huntington Park, South Gate, Lincoln Heights, East Los

Angeles, and Alhambra. The majority lives within the jurisdiction of the El Sereno neighborhood. The scope of this study encompasses the story of El Sereno because it is a rich example of a place where a schooling community, in the midst of a rich cultural legacy, comes together to teach and learn. In addition, this study is focused on the intersections of AP and CS schooling because El Sereno's prominent Mesoamerican presence serves as a promising site to study the formation of a learning community that incorporates a foundation of AP in a CS classroom.

There are several examples of efforts in El Sereno to incorporate AP, but none has focused on CS. These examples include Academia Semillas del Pueblo Charter School Xinaxcalmecac (K-8th), Anahuacalmecac International University Preparatory High School of North America, The Eastside Café, the El Sereno Community Garden, and the Barrio Action Youth and Family Center. I offer a brief introduction to each of these.

In 2002, a charter school community materialized a schooling indigenous presence by founding Academia Semillas del Pueblo Charter School Xinaxcalmecac (K-8th) on Huntington Drive, one of El Sereno's main streets. Semillas serves children of the area and its surrounding communities, and continues to grow every year. This school has received International Baccalaureate recognition for its appreciation and incorporation of the cultural and intellectual heritage of Native American Peoples, while also promoting positive social awareness.

In September 2008, Anahuacalmecac International University Preparatory High School of North America was established a couple of blocks from the first campus, utilizing El Sereno's old library space. This provided a continuation of the schooling community begun at Semillas.

Xocolatl, a school-based project cultural coffeehouse of Xinaxcalmecac, was established in 2009 as a social enterprise to help the schooling families of the schools inspired by the self-sustainability of the Zapatista movement. Xocolatl Café served indigenous drinks made with cacao beans, which have been used to make ceremonial drinks. The campuses and café perpetuated an indigenous presence through their aromas of food, the institutionalization and preservation of the Nahuatl language, the sounding of the huehuetl[11] during ancient Danza practices, and the bright ancient colors that reflect those in the natural world in the images. These serve to reinforce a collective ancestral identity that permeates the memories of those who walk these lands to and from their schools.

A few blocks from the Semillas Community Schools is another establishment on Huntington Drive that serves as a cultural space: The Eastside Café. It is an educational space founded by El Sereno residents for the evolvement of sustainable self-reliance through education, cultural awareness, health, and the arts. It is a space where people come together to engage in activities that promote long-term community development through an active and conscious citizenship and a renewed positive collective identity. "As an [autonomous] organization, the Eastside Café relies on its members and the grassroots community for monetary support" to sustain the space while deliberately rejecting outside dependence on grants and government funds because it is grounded in the mission that

> all people and all communities have the right to self-governance and self-determination and that we possess within our own communities all the knowledge and power to make this a reality. We are not involved in a struggle for power: we possess the power already and are working to create a positive alternative to the negatives of our present situation. (Eastside Café organizing committee, 2010, September 19)

The cultural space is driven by eight principles, which are worth noting, in order to give the reader the context of this study, which is situated within a community of long-term consciousness building and activism. The following is incorporated into the Eastside Café Echospace' vision statement, which can be found at their website.[12]

1. We believe another world is possible only if we, the grassroots, the majority, play a key role in building it.
2. We believe in community-based organizing that is independent, pluriethnic and asset-based (as opposed to deficit-based). We rely on who we are and what we can do.
3. We believe that we are all equal because we are all different and difference is essential to our unique contribution. Respect for the different nature and role of each is law.
4. We believe in participatory democracy and will strive to use consensus for decision-making.
5. We believe that key to building participatory democracy is rebuilding respect, solidarity, and mutual self-help.

6. We believe that government laws, while they can at times help, don't make us free—we are the only ones that can free ourselves.
7. We believe that we all have the obligation and ability to lead in something and therefore there should be no special status or privileges given to leaders. We are all leaders. We are all special.
8. We believe in developing autonomous, alternative, moral economy that allows for the dignified development of the human potential.

The Eastside Café is also a political space of renewed self-determination, one that relies on our community cultural wealth as the foundation of our learning and acting in the world. The creation of this space was influenced by a group of young activists who worked with the Zapatista Indigenous Peoples of Chiapas, Mexico, in 1994, during their resistance to neoliberal policies that, under the Clinton administration, opened free trade under NAFTA. This agreement, a neoliberal policy aimed to decrease poverty rates and living expenses in Mexico by eliminating tariffs on imports to the United States. The indigenous people of Mexico knew that this policy was the continuation of a dominant force that controls farmers' produce in Mexico. In short, activists visiting from El Sereno witnessed first-hand the negative effects of US policies and were determined to bring home an alternative for self-governance and collective action through exercising our collective identity and action.

Shortly after the Eastside Café was established, the El Sereno Community Garden sprouted across the street, just south of the Eastside Café on Huntington Drive. After advocating for the Caltrans-owned[13] space to bring down the fence that had stood since 1996, a group of residents successfully obtained permission to cultivate the space as a positive community growth of social relations, herbs, vegetables, and fruit in 2004. Since then, a group of residents continues to work the land and hold community meetings and cultural activities for residents to enjoy.

Finally, another example I wish to highlight of El Sereno's vibrant community cultural wealth is Barrio Action Youth and Family Center, an establishment sponsored by the City of Los Angeles in partnership with other governmental organizations, such as the Children's Bureau of Southern California, the Los Angeles County Departments of Children and Family Services, and Mental and Public Health, and the Los Angeles Unified School District, among others. The center's purpose is to commune with young people and their families so that they can make life choices that will help them personally, academically, and socially. It is a space where community members come together to work toward creating and sustaining a healthy social and physical lifestyle.

El Sereno is a 4.17-square-mile northeastern neighborhood of Los Angeles, adjacent to City Terrace, Lincoln Heights, South Pasadena, and Alhambra. In 2008, according to the Los Angeles Department of City Planning, 43,766 people called El Sereno their home (*LA Times*, 2010). This city boasts a population of predominantly Mexican foreign-born ancestry (65.8%). It is ranked as the 28th most Mesoamerican-descent-populated neighborhood of Los Angeles, with East Los Angeles (96.7%) and Boyle Heights (94%), two as its neighboring municipalities, rank first and fifth as the most Mesoamerican-populated neighborhoods (of 272 neighborhoods) in Los Angeles, respectively.

Although Los Angeles continues to be a place of plurality of knowledges, its systemic neoliberal policies remain a colonial practice that systematically prefers a dominant, standardized way of thinking and acting in the world. Yet the lived experiences of nondominant populations rise above concrete jungles with deepening historical roots that provide the substance of our increased mobilization and perseverance in these lands.

El Sereno is one protagonist of this story because it is the little piece of earth that brings together a wealth of community knowledge that will be detailed in the following chapters. By reading this account, I invite you to take a small part of a worldview as it is told through my eyes, my voice, and my fingers as I type away in this sacred nest of El Sereno.

However, the fundamental reason I chose El Sereno as the nexus of my work is because my roots run deep here. Five generations of my paternal family have lived here, since 1957. I was hecha en Zacatecas, México, and I was born here after I crossed the border as an 18-week-old fetus, as my mom hid in the trunk of a car. We lived my first formative years with my grandmother, and then we moved to Alhambra, where I attended public school until I completed the 8th grade. Throughout my high school years, my parents and siblings would take the ten-minute journey at least twice a week down Huntington Drive to visit my grandmother, aunts, and cousins. It is this rinconcito de tierra[14] that I consider when I make connections to the lively experiences of preserving a culture through familial gatherings around food, with a unique form of communication that we trace back to our place of origin—Los Morales, El Cargadero, La Colonia Benito Juárez, and Huejucar—all ranchos near the municipality of Jerez, Zacatecas, that cradle my family lineage. The depth and breadth of my family roots in this neighborhood of El Sereno have powerful implications for the people that currently reside in this place. We take part in communal living. On this one hill alone, our family lives in five of approximately thirty houses, and we have relationships of forty years or more with a good number of our neighbors. We grew up witnessing each other's growth very closely, eating, communing over challenges, and celebrating years together. My grandmother remains en la casa grande,[15] and I have moved to live within twelve houses from her on the same loma[16] that I've frequented since I was born. This forms an ideal space for my inquiry around the community's cultural wealth, as it relates to schooling practices. I consider El Sereno my paternal family nest in this country. My positionality informs the decisions I have made and continue to make about what I study, how I study it, whom it benefits, and how I present my findings.

Through my exploration of the macro context, I discuss the following questions: How may student-led initiatives and classroom practices inform a neighborhood-wide schooling movement toward educational excellence and general wellness? How do AP and CS interact in this macro space? What role does the Lomas High School Garden Collective have in creating spaces that promote positive academic and cultural identities for *all students*? What implications does this study have for other contexts?

3.9   Data Collection and Analysis

This book focuses on the building of a learning foundation in a CS classroom that is multicultural and relevant to the lives of students' families, homes, and communities. This research is conducted with sanctity. At its core is an accountability to relationships with students' families, homes, and communities, to the extent possible for and constrained by the limitations of the researcher. Its approach is participatory as well as communal in the making, with all its constraints and affordances. Therefore, the data collection of this study will focus on three general areas: a single CS classroom, the Lomas High Schooling Community, and the El Sereno Home Community. In the classroom, I look at student artifacts, which include final projects in two units, specifically, and conduct a discourse analysis of the project presentations offered by student groups. In addition, I look closely at the answers to end-of-unit surveys that students completed about their participation and learning in that unit. I also analyze the focus group interviews conducted at the end of the school year about their participation and learning in ECS throughout the year, with special attention paid to the social science behind the field of CS, identity, community connections, and AP.

This cycle of planning, doing, checking, acting, and inquiring represents the tenants of participatory action research (Camarrota & Fine, 2008) and of appropriate accountability to relationships, as invoked by an indigenous research paradigm that pays explicit attention to reciprocity and family-like relationships. The CS classroom can be the source of looking back as much as looking forward, as students who learn CS see themselves in the curriculum, and think of themselves and act in relation to their families and communities. After all, the premise of this study is to remember the ancient to imagine and create something new with all of our relations in mind, heart, body, and spirit. The following sections describe the data more fully.

3.10   Lomas High School

Nestled atop the characteristic rolling hills of El Sereno, Lomas High School is one of the oldest campuses in Los Angeles Unified School District. It first opened its doors in 1937 at the present-day El Sereno Middle School site. In 1970, Lomas moved to its current location on the hill. The school was originally built on a mule farm, hence its choice for mascot as the mule. In addition, Lomas's association with the democratic party confirmed for Lomas that the mule was an appropriate mascot for the school. Student activism has a historic presence at Lomas.

I will begin Chapter 4 with the initiatives that a group of students across campus took to resurrect MEChA, a student-led organization at Lomas. The spark that the students created motivated other students and supportive adults, including teachers, the researcher, and parents, to respond to their desire to (a) promote cultural awareness, (b) connect to the community at large, and (c) support university pathways. I analyze the co-construction of these common visions with other organizations on campus, like the Parent Center, an interdisciplinary team of teachers (which includes the CS teacher), and a nonprofit social justice organization, the Asian Pacific American Legal Center[17] (APALC), whose participation has been vital to the development of informal and formal spaces of learning. The purpose of beginning the gathering of data in the informal yet influential spaces across the high school campus at the microlevel was to inform the context of this study, as this space helps construct the content that influences the formal space of the CS classroom, which is detailed in Chapter 5. The general question explored at the microlevel is: *How may student inquiry co-influence positive collective identities and agencies for communal wellness, including educational excellence?*

3.10.1   MEChA

I collected audio and video recordings of MEChA meetings twice a week. In addition, I kept a journal in which I recorded notes from all the meetings. These meetings included: (a) weekly off-campus meetings of core members at a local establishment, (b) weekly on-campus student-body meetings, (c) Mesoamerican Studies workshop meetings twice a month, and (d) weekly Danza[18] meetings over the last four months of the academic school year. At the end of the 2010–2011 academic year, students' personal statements for college entry were also analyzed.

3.10.2   Parent Center

The Parent Center at Lomas High School hosted several events that included the participation of MEChA and classes that are part of the Lomas High School Garden Collective. It was common for the Parent Center to host workshops about making tortillas a mano. Although the office did not fund the necessary materials needed for these workshops, the parents, mostly mothers, would bring various ingredients and tools for the making of hand-made corn tortillas. Another event that was popular is a trueque, an activity that reintroduced a model for bargaining practices or items. This event was the most popular, drawing parents from neighboring schools. Field notes of four of these key events throughout the year are analyzed with open, axial, and selective coding to dovetail the figured world of MEChA's identity formation and participation.

3.11   COMPUTER SCIENCE CLASSROOM

At the microlevel, I will use Scratch to examine learning opportunities for students to develop their understanding of CS through the programming unit, the results of which will be offered in Chapter 5. Scratch is an interactive animation program.[19] Specifically, I will address the questions raised at this level through the question: *How do participants make sense of and act on AP and CS intersections over time?*

3.11.1   Field Notes and Student Artifacts

I collected data that were documented during the six-week program-ming units from April 2–June 7, 2011, and again from September 28–October 25, 2011. The unit focuses on smaller projects that scaffold learning parts of programming an animated piece using Scratch, such as a game or a story. Both units are compared to identify the differences between the second year of observation, during which AP was infused into the curriculum, and the first year, when AP was not included. To do this, I examine field notes from site visits and student artifacts. The student artifacts were results of the culminating task of the unit. They were used to tell stories about their community's strengths and weaknesses, including the challenges in their neighborhood and discus-sion of ways to empower viewers to use their agency to make changes in their neighborhoods. This unit is a rich data source because it is a time and space in which students have the ability to explore a topic of choice, tell a powerful story about it as a way to raise conscious-ness within a community, and inspire action through their animated projects.

3.11.2   The Computer Science Male Teacher of European-descent

This teacher was selected because, like the mainstream teaching profes-sion that serves students of color in CS, the teacher's background does not reflect the cultural make-up of his students. Therefore, if this study is to prove useful to a wide range of teachers, it is important to look at the most challenging (and all too common) case. This involved working with a teacher who was not trained in culturally relevant pedagogy, yet who aspires to engage students in his classroom while promoting creativ-ity, as well as algorithmic problem-solving methods.[20] Allan identifies as a European-descent male teacher who was trained in chemistry, business, and CS. These are fields that have been traditionally devoid of social jus-tice and culturally responsive, relevant pedagogy. As Allan began to teach ECS, he was coupled with an ECS coach who guided his reflection about his teaching practices during frequent lunch period meetings throughout the school year. These reflections were audio-recorded and transcribed, coded, and reported here to demonstrate Allan's thinking about his prac-tice over time.

3.11.3   Students

Twelve of twenty-two students were asked to participate in end-of-the-year reflections based upon their participation in the class. Participation was based on their level of engagement in the completion of their final projects. The criteria used to measure engagement included: Did they complete their assignments? Did they ask for help when they needed it? Did they choose a topic to focus on during their final Scratch projects? Did they pay special attention to the Scratch unit? All students were "engaged" at one point or another, and all students articulated the storyboard they were visualizing for their final Scratch project, but not all of them finished on time or maximized their time in class. I selected six students who finished their Scratch projects during class or after school and six students who had not finished their Scratch projects, either because they needed more time or because they were not "motivated" to complete it in the time allotted. This grouping of students was done in an effort to collect data that more accurately reflected the entire population of the students in this class. Of the twelve students selected, one student opted out of participation in the reflection. The other eleven students met at different times with the ECS coach and me to discuss their experiences and learning in the class.

3.11.4   Student Notebooks

The notebooks were kept throughout the school year, during each of the six units, and were provided by Mr. Adams at the beginning of the year. The students recorded their general reflections about the class and learning in response to the teacher's daily warm-up questions on the whiteboard. The notebooks were analyzed to explore student engagement throughout the year.

3.12   EL SERENO SCHOOLING COMMUNITY

The influence that both the micro- and the meso-level have on the schooling community of El Sereno at large will be described in Chapter 6. In order to focus on the role that these more fine-grained levels have on the macro context of a neighborhood, I look at events open to the community at large that specifically took place at Lomas High School. I also look at the ways in which the neighborhood co-constructed AP and CS practices where they intersect at the school. In order to do this, I explore the following question: *How may student-led initiatives and classroom practices inform a neighborhood-wide schooling movement towards general wellness, including educational excellence?*

3.12.1   *Teacher-Initiated Inquiry Project (TIIP) (2010–2012)*[21]

From MEChA's teacher and researcher engagement came the idea to apply for a grant that would support our vision, which we entitled, "DietSens: Mobilize ancestral memory, advanced technology and student inquiry for health in our community and high school of El Sereno." I focused my data collection on the DietSens campaign (more details in Chapter 5) of the Period 6 Collaborative,[22] which includes over 1500 responses to mobile surveys using participatory sensing—data collection via mobile technology—around food and drink practices of three participating classes in TIIP, a transdisciplinary collaboration of three areas of discipline. As recipients of the grant, we formalized our collaborations with APALC, ECS, and MEChA to form the campus-wide Lomas High School Garden Collective, culminating our efforts in the *The People's Garden Planting Festival.* To date The People's Garden continues to grow.

3.12.2   *The Healthy Start Fair Community Presentation*

The fair was an event organized by the Healthy Start Office of Los Angeles Unified School District, along with two other El Sereno schools: El Sereno Middle School and Farmdale Elementary. Although this fair had been conducted for six years prior to May 2011, it had never taken place at Lomas High School, one of the three schools included in the preparation and hosting of the event. For the first time, Lomas High School hosted the Healthy Start Fair on its campus. This is significant because elementary and middle school families joined in the planning and participation of this event at the high school. The ceremony began at sunrise with a ceremony by Don Guillermo, parent coordinator at all three schools. I have chosen to include this event because students in ECS presented their final Scratch presentations to the larger community at this time. I documented the responses that the community, students, researchers, and teacher had to the event, and I will describe these in Chapters 5 and 6 as an example of a connection to the community that a CS class can have and the impact this experience had on schooling participants. This analysis is done through video analysis and coding on the day of the event.

Returning to the grounded theory approach, I use open, axial, and selective coding, as advanced by Strauss and Corbin (1990). Grounded theory provides a procedure for developing categories of information, such as open coding, interconnectedness between categories, or axial coding, and building a story that connects the categories in selective coding. During the open coding phase, I examined the text (e.g., transcripts, field notes, documents, student artifacts) for common themes that I then developed into categories.

Once an initial set of categories was developed through a process of extrapolating specific properties of set categories, I turned to axial coding, which is entwined with the foundational research question: How may Mesoamerican academic cultural practices provide a foundation for a positive learning ecology of cultural academic identities in three organizational levels of a public high school, especially in spaces that have been historically segregated, like CS education? Axial coding was useful for conducting a coding paradigm that visually portrayed the interrelationships of these codes to the general constructs of the study. Finally, I selectively coded any influences that arose as I analyzed the actions of participants. The most prevalent themes resulted in the following chapters and topics of this book. For instance, results show that students have suggested the need to incorporate families into the activities of the curriculum throughout the year. I plan to look at the suggestions that students have made more closely and to continue the dialog with Allan and the coach[23] for ECS at Lomas High School. For example, what are the students saying about the curriculum or pedagogy? What have they enjoyed? What have they learned? I propose to help inform the re-creation and implementation of the ECS class for the next academic year. As you can see, this study is not separated from praxis. It is as intimately tied to inquiry and theoretical underpinnings as it is to the relationships and actions with students, curriculum, the teacher, the coach, and so forth.

3.13   LIMITATIONS

One of the most common criticisms of narratology is that this approach narrowly focuses on the individual over the social context. Although what brought the study together was a focus on individual activities among a small set of high school students, I look at three organizational schooling levels to acknowledge and address this limitation.

This study applies to a very constrained area of El Sereno: a single high school and a single high school classroom. Although the great strength of this study lies in my personal connections to this community and the interconnectedness between three organizational levels of schooling, this is also potentially the greatest challenge, as it makes it more difficult to obtain "objectivity" and, therefore, to uncover the overall possibility of generalizing the findings of this research.

Another constraint of the study lies in attempting to capture the influence of a relatively new curriculum. There can be no comparison done with a class of students in a more traditional introduction to CS simply because ECS is a prototypical curriculum; in fact, it never existed before. The first iteration of the curriculum began in 2009 with five teachers.

When highlighting AP practices, one can easily slide down the slippery slope of romanticizing the past or focusing so much on the past that today's issues become irrelevant. I am not placing AP as a confluence of religious practices. AP is *not* a religion, but rather a worldview—not to be confused and placed in a framework that is familiar to us, an institutional practice of religion. Human behavior is similar in many cultures. Overall, humans have more commonalities than differences. The same holds true for our practices, ancient and current, that engage with similar forces in nature.

NOTES

1. Connelly and Clandinin (2006) situate Narrative Inquiry in three commonplaces that are explored simultaneously: temporality, space, and sociality. This approach is especially useful in the classroom space as a context encapsulates multiple dimensions of study, considering the teacher, student, content, and the milieu of curriculum.
2. Movimiento Estudiantil Chican@s de Aztlán. MEChA is a national student-led organization that was born in the 1960s during the Chican@ Movement. http://www.nationalmecha.org/.
3. Day of the Dead, with roots in ancient Mesoamerica.

4. Greetings. My family's custom is to *pasar a saludar a los mayores*, or make some time to visit the elderly, even if it means just to say hello.
5. Don is term that indicates respect of an elder.
6. P'urhépecha peoples are original to the Mexican state of Michoacán.
7. Positive Action.
8. Scratch is a two-dimensional drag-and-drop programming environment created by MIT to ""lower the floor" for programming, so that children could get started earlier. In our view, learning to program is somewhat like learning to write. In both cases, children should start as soon as they are interested. It makes sense for children to start with simple forms of expression, and gradually learn more subtle and sophisticated ways of expressing themselves over time" (Utting et al., 2010, p. 17:2). Scratch is often used to create games. http://scratch.mit.edu/.
9. UCLA Center X is a comprehensive organization that extends across two graduate credential programs and professional development projects whose dedication is to build public schooling to create a "more just, equitable and humane society". http://centerx.gseis.ucla.edu/
10. DietSens is a participatory sensing campaign that uses mobile technology to document the food and drink practices of participants in the study. More detailed information can be found in Chapter 5.
11. "The huehuetl is a percussion instrument from Mexico, used by the Aztecs and other cultures. It is an upright tubular drum made from a wooden body opened at the bottom that stands on three legs cut from its base, with skin stretched over the top. It can be beaten by hand or wood mallet. The instrument's size varies from the minor *huehuetl* to the medium *panhuehuetl* and to the major *tlalpanhuehuetl*" (http://en.wikipedia.org/wiki/Huehuetl).
12. http://4.bp.blogspot.com/_VMk-v_1GBpY/SaoD4RKaDqI/AAAAAAAAANM/6raNE5hoO84/s1600-h/vision+statement.jpg.
13. Caltrans is the California Department of Transportation.
14. Corner of land.
15. In the big house.
16. Knoll.
17. http://www.apalc.org/.
18. Danza is commonly referred to as 'Aztec Dancing'. Its practice has a long history that dates pre-colonial times.
19. http://scratch.mit.edu/.
20. Algorithmic problem-solving is a step-by-step process used during the problem-solving process and constitutes one of the units of focus in the ECS curriculum used in class.
21. The TIIP grant was a project by UCLA Center X, Los Angeles Unified School District and UCLA College of Letters of Science and awarded by

California Postsecondary Education Commission. The goal of the project was to promote teacher creativity in their schools with a vision of social justice.
22. Our TIIP grant was a collaborative effort between ECS, Chicanx Studies and Leadership Development in Interethnic Relations. The three courses coincidentally met during sixth period of the school day. On occasions, the three classes would meet for student collaboration.
23. As part of the ECS program, the teacher is supported by a coach who regularly visits the CS class for collaboration, reflection on instruction, and consulting.

REFERENCES

Anonymous. (2010, August 6). Mapping Los Angeles: El Sereno. *Los Angeles Times*. Retrieved from http://projects.latimes.com/mapping-la/neighborhoods/neighborhood/el-sereno/.

Brown, A. (1992). Design experiments: Theoretical and methodological challenges in creating complex interventions in classroom settings. *The Journal of the Learning Sciences, 2*(2), 141–178.

Camarrota, J., & Fine, M. (2008). *Revolutionizing education: Youth participatory action research in motion*. New York, NY: Routledge.

Chrystos. (1983). I walk in the history of my people. In G. Anzaldúa & C. Moraga (Eds.), *This bridge called my back: Writings by radical women of color*. New York, NY: Kitchen Table.

Clandinin, D. J., & Connelly, F. M. (1988). Studying teachers' knowledge of classrooms: Collaborative research, ethics and the negotiation of narrative. *The Journal of Educational Thought, 22*(2A), 269–282.

Connelly, F. M., & Clandinin, D. J. (1990). Stories of experience and narrative inquiry. *Educational Researcher, 19*(5), 2–14.

Connelly, F. M., & Clandinin, D. J. (2006). Narrative inquiry. In J. L. Green, G. Camilli, & P. B. Elmore (Eds.), *Handbook of complimentary methods in education research* (pp. 477–487). Washington, DC: American Educational Research Association.

DataQuest. (2010). Educational Demographics Unit. Retrieved February 16, 2010, from California Department of Education.

Delgado Bernal, D. (1998, Winter). Using Chicana feminist epistemology in educational research. *Harvard Educational Review, 68*(4), 555–582.

Delgado Bernal, D., Alejandra Elenes, C., Godinez, F. E., & Villenas, S. (Eds.). (2006). *Chicana/Latina education in everyday life: Feminista perspectives on pedagogy and epistemology*. Albany: State University of New York Press.

Lomas, J. (2007). The in-between world of knowledge brokering. *British Medical Journal, 334,* 129–132.

Eastside Café Organizing Committee. (2010, September 19). *Welcome to the Eastside Café!* Available at http://eastsidecafeechospace.blogspot.com/.

Gonzáles, P., & Rodríguez, R. (2005). *Amoxtli san ce tojuan: We are one— nosotros somos uno.* San Fernando, CA: Xicano Records and Film. Wallerstein (1991, 2003).

Holland, D., & Lachiotte, W., Jr. (1998). *Identity and agency in cultural worlds.* Cambridge, MA: Harvard University Press.

Howard, T. (2003). Culturally relevant pedagogy: Ingredients for critical teacher reflection. *Theory into Practice, 42*(3), 195–202.

Kelly, A. (2004). Design research in education: Yes, but is it methodological? *Journal of the Learning Sciences, 13*(1), 115–128.

Lewin, K. (1946). Action research and minority problems. *Journal of Social Issues, 2*(4), 34–46.

Mander, J. (1992). *In the absence of the sacred: The failure of technology and the survival of the Indian Nations.* San Francisco, CA: Sierra Club Books.

Moreno Sandoval, C. D., Mojica Lagunas, R., Montelongo, L., & Díaz, M. (2016). Ancestral knowledge systems: A conceptual framework for decolonizing research in social science. *AlterNative: An International Journal of Indigenous Peoples, 12*(1), 18–31.

Martínez, E. (2009). *500 years of Chicana women's history, 500 años de la mujer chicana.* New Brunswick, NJ: Rutgers University Press.

Morrell, E. (2008). *Critical literacy and urban youth: Pedagogies of access, dissent, and liberation.* New York, NY: Routledge.

Nasir, N. I. S., & Hand, V. (2006). Exploring sociocultural perspectives on race, culture, and learning. *American Educational Research Association, 76*(4), 449–475.

Orfield, G., Losen, D., Wald, J., & Swanson, C. B. (2004). *Losing our future: How minority youth are being left behind by the graduation rate crisis.* Cambridge: The Civil Rights Project at Harvard University.

Quijano, A. (2000). Coloniality of Power and Eurocentrism in Latin America. *International Sociology, 15*(2), 215–232.

Rogers, J., Bertrand, M., Freelon, R., & Fanelli, S. (2011). *California educational opportunity.* Los Angeles, CA: UCLA's Institute for Democracy, Education, and Access.

Sfard, A., & Prusak, A. (2005). Telling identities: In search of an analyitic tool for investigating learning as a culturally shaped activity. *Educational Researcher, 34*(4), 14–22.

Smith, L. T. (1999). *Decolonizing methodologies: Research and indigenous peoples.* London: Zed Books.

Solorzano, D. G., & Yosso, T. J. (2002). A critical race counterstory of race, racism, and affirmative action. *Equity & Excellence in Education, 35,* 155–168. University of Massachusetts School of Education Journal.

Strauss, A., & Corbin, J. (1990). *Basics of qualitative research: Grounded theory procedures and techniques.* Newbury Park, CA: Sage.

Utting, I., Cooper, S., Kölling, M., Maloney, J., & Resnick, M. (2010, November). Alice, greenfoot and scratch—A discussion. *ACM Transactions on Computing Education 10*(4), Article 17, 11 pages. http://doi.acm.org/10.1145/1868358.1868364.

Vaughan, D. (2002). Signals of interpretive work: The role of culture in a theory of practical action. In K. A. Cerulo (Ed.), *Culture in mind: Toward a sociology of culture and cognition* (pp. 28–54). New York: Routledge.

Yosso, T. (2005). Whose culture has capital? A critical race theory discussion of community cultural wealth. *Race Ethnicity and Education, 8*(1), 69–91.

CHAPTER 4

Critical Self-Consciousness for Collective Action in Social Commonplace: *Building a Sustainable Environment for Planting Seeds of Hope*, 2009–2010

In this chapter, we explore **germinating critical consciousness** and academic success in computing education. Since critical consciousness originates from the self, and radiates outward, we begin with things we don't realize that we know, then build toward things we know we know, but might be wrong about, and continue outward toward things we know we don't know, and wish to learn.

In this fairly new territory of **cultivating cultural identities as academic practices**, we examine the intersections between **confidence, leadership**, and **cultural competence** through the lens of computer science.

We also explore **teaching computing as a form of activism,** and begin to consider longer-term ramifications of more tailored educational experiences that take individual perspectives into account, not merely by accident, but as a matter of course.

When a spider weaves her web, she knows how to whirl the fiber from her spinners to make the perfect manta for the day. She wasn't *taught* how to do it, she just *knows how*; it is part of her instinctual survival mechanism. What would happen if her world were turned upside down and her survival strategies suddenly did "not fit" into her environment?

Similarly, adolescents *know how* to thrive within a community, as long as the community knows how to make space for the reverberating creativity and intellectual leadership of youth today. Unfortunately, at a systemic macro-level, we have not been able to sustain a positive ecology in public

© The Author(s) 2019   87
C. D. M. Sandoval, *Ancestral Knowledge Meets Computer Science Education*, Postcolonial Studies in Education,
https://doi.org/10.1057/978-1-137-47520-6_4

schools for young people to develop themselves as recognized builders of our nations. As a result, teens often feel ostracized, silenced, or unfit in the institutions that were once idealized as a space to promote a demo-cratic approach to living and learning. But what happens when these same schooling institutions denigrate the historical knowledge of underrepre-sented young people, as demonstrated by Arizona's recent suspension of ethnic studies with the passing of Arizona House Bill 2281? Young people nonetheless cut through concrete jungles and show themselves sprouting, as dignified as the delicate spider weaving her web. Educational reform must begin with young people's *palabra*, a method of expression as they imagine our future before we, as adults, co-construct this vision.

The focus of this study is to bridge socio-historical ways of knowing to modern uses of digital science so that we can engage in a dialectical praxis of el vivir comunitario. El vivir is a vision that rings true for com-munities throughout the central and southern parts of the Western hem-isphere. It refers to a myriad of spiritual, economic, political, emotional, historical, and social decolonizing systems, resisting a coloniality of power (Grosfoguel, 2010; Quijano, 2000). The decolonizing approach of el vivir comunitario unwinds hierarchical systems of power toward dig-nified ways of living, learning, and dying. I will later include a deeper discussion of el vivir as it comes to life in this chapter.

For now, I will analyze student activism as it extends across three organizational levels: micro- to meso- to macro-environments that span institutional and non-institutional spaces, beginning with the microcosm of a student-led organization. I will *purposely* avoid a discussion of com-puter science learning in this chapter, to counter the common techno-philia (an obsession with technology without a critical analysis of its use and the way in which digital tools affect human relationships [Turkle, 2011]) that is used to exult digital science as a savior for just about any societal problem. With this narrow and often dangerous approach, we often act from a glamorizing perception of digital tools as a sexy advance-ment in problem-solving. Instead, I propose that we think critically about the historical uses of this technology and question whether it is appropri-ate to use in a specific context. I explore the ways in which students mobi-lize themselves *outside* of the technophilia craze and later (in Chapter 5), I show how computer science learning intersects with Itzel's ancestral praxis within the meso-space of the *Exploring Computer Science* classroom.

In this thoughtfully designed micro-space of student organization, we note the pronounced creativity and intellectual merit that teens collectively use to build a common vision of sustainable ecologies that crosses cultural differences and political ideologies. While socio-cultural theorists define informal spaces of learning as a third space, I use the term *nepantla* (Anzaldúa, 1987) here as an indicator of spatial continuities that cross classroom, outdoor, and community spaces where learning takes place. In addition, nepantla serves as a transitory space that allows participants to experience living in la frontera, a space that nurtures flexibility to a relational construction to defining the self. These spaces sustained a high level of commitment by the participants: students, educators, parents, community members, and myself. My participation served multiple purposes, ranging from a resident with family ties in El Sereno to a researcher activist and an invited sponsor for the student-led organization. As such, I take full responsibility for my careful design of words and actions. I wholeheartedly trust that you, as critical and creative readers, will engage with us in dialogue toward el vivir comunitario. I presume that you, too, will assume responsibility as active participants in the weaving of our nations.

Using a Narrative Inquiry approach that weaves the findings of the research study into discussions along the way, the following pages illustrate a process that high school students have diligently co-created, a vibrant woven fabric within a dialectic. This dialectic serves as a unifying palpitation of concentric circles of worlds that bleed into each other, a web of complexity that breathes life into our communities, into our homes. Although there are many players involved in this community of practice, I follow student inquiry by walking alongside Itzel in her journey. She resisted joining MEChA in the beginning, but eventually she developed leadership skills that brought her the initiative to enroll in *Exploring Computer Science* in 2011. We will bear witness to the reflexive practices in the social commonplace students develop as they uncover consciousness *together* and what they construct with their newfound awareness. We will see how high school students take their learning to the next level by involving *familia*. Herein begins the first year of documented co-influence of student inquiry on campus-wide organizational identity and agency toward el vivir comunitario throughout a comprehensive public high school in El Sereno.

4.1   CIRCLING AROUND THE FIRE WITH A PURPOSE

"Dora kept asking me to go to the meetings of a club...." Itzel describes her first encounters with MEChA, directed by her good-friend-like-a-sister, Dora. She knew about MEChA from her cousin, who was involved in MEChA at another high school, but she never really "drew attention" to the organization "until Día de los Muertos." Itzel was hearing the buzz surrounding the planning of Día de los Muertos assembly. There were only two weeks ahead of them, so they were acting quickly, organizing during and after school in various spaces on and off campus. They were to put on a program that centered historical cultural practices to a larger group of students, campus-wide.

Although Itzel did not take her friend's advice to join MEChA the first time, she was most impacted by the presence of *danzantes*[1] when she attended the assembly with her Advanced Placement English class, "cuz my dad was a danzante." She was invited to join the Danza circle during the school-wide assembly. This experience left an impression on her because it opened up the possibility of "uniting with others." She later realized that her participation in Danza re-opened a connection with her father. Participating in Danza at school was the turning point for her involvement in the organization. She accepted her friend's invitation to join the club immediately after the assembly: "So I went to all the meetings they had to plan for...how to start MEChA...and it was only like eight or nine of us, but all of us were committed. So I felt we had a really strong group...." Itzel refers to MEChA as a "strong group" that was "committed."

I will describe how this strong group planted seeds of hope in fertile soil, a figured world of ancestral praxis that extends across spatial commonplaces. In the center of this world is the centripetal force of student activism and adult support, a fire that names our shared historical cultural practices as a collective identity that feeds our dignity in critical and reflexive ways. This community of practice within *nepantla* holds the fire that maintains a movement toward el vivir comunitario alive.

While there are many players in our communal effort to build a positive learning ecology for el vivir comunitario, Table 4.1 introduces a sample of the participants included in this chapter, in alphabetical order.

In 2009, a group of students was inspired by their Mexican American Studies class to resurrect a student-led organization, MEChA, on their high school campus. They came together during the Fall 2009 semester

Table 4.1 Schooling participants mentioned in this chapter

Name	Age in 2010 ‖ Sex	Role (cm = community member)
Alberto	35, male	Semillas del Pueblo single parent, cm
Carolina	53, female	Lomas High School single parent of 4, cm
Cueponcaxochitl	30, female	Lomas High School MEChA sponsor, cm
Cynthia	17, female	MEChA mesa member, co-chair
Dora	16, female	MEChA mesa member, co-chair
Elisa	16, female	MEChA mesa member
Elmer	16, male	MEChA mesa member
Itzel	16, female	MEChA mesa member
Ivan	16, male	MEChA mesa member
Jason	17, male	MEChA mesa member
Jose	34, male	Eastside Café volunteer, cm
Josué	16, male	MEChA mesa member
Lesly	30, male	Asian Pacific American Legal Center Fellow
Mr. Ambrocio	31, male	Lomas High School educator
Mr. Armenta	29, male	Lomas High School educator
Mr. Dueñas	31, male	Lomas High School educator, MEChA sponsor, cm
Mr. Floragon	31, male	Lomas High School educator, MEChA sponsor, cm
Quetzal	8, male	Semillas del Pueblo student
Raul	52, male	Cm
Tocatzin	32, male	LACMA Educator in Mesoamerica, cm
Xochitl	16, female	MEChA mesa member
Xochitl	24, female	Older sister to Dora and Cynthia, cm

to organize a school-wide assembly for Día de los Muertos, an ancient celebration of life and death with origins in Mesoamerica, now infused with European *mestizaje* (Anzaldúa, 1987). With teacher support, Dora, a junior at the time in Mexican American Studies with Mr. Dueñas, jump-started the mobilization of students. She single-handedly recruited a group of students to participate in the organization of a school-wide assembly. What began as a seemingly ordinary effort to present a school assembly turned into something with greater significance. Dora's push (with Mr. Dueñas' full support) inspired eight other students to commit themselves to re-instituting MEChA beyond Día de los Muertos. After several meetings with Mr. Dueñas and Mr. Floragon, they settled on three goals for the group: (1) promote cultural awareness, (2) connect to the community, and (3) advance college-going rates. The tending of this community nurtured our sense of belonging to something that spoke to our generational worldviews, language practices, colorful schemes in foods, dress, and family inclusion. Our community represented a figured world that continues to sprout up throughout the land with groups that are interested in learning more about our shared ancestral praxis systems.

Sobonfu Somé (1999) described the role of community best in her book, *The spirit of intimacy*: "Community is the spirit, the guiding light of the tribe, whereby people come together in order to fulfill a specific purpose, to help others fulfill their purpose, and to take care of one another" (p. 65). Raised in Burkina Faso, away from "the states," Somé detailed the ways in which she experienced communal living, o el vivir comunitario, within its own complex systems. She explained that the goal of a community "is to make sure that each member of the community is heard" and given an opportunity to share his/her practices. Each member contributes their practice, for "without these [practices], the community dies. And without the community, the individual is left without a place where they can contribute" (p. 65).

Itzel noticed that a strong community is comprised of dedicated individuals. She recognized that one is "passionate" when one can relate to others and share her "energy into something that is worth it." The community becomes a matrix of temporal, spatial, and social commonplace, a practice that envelops a figured world that sustains itself through its participants, a praxis of meaning-making by collective dialogue and action.

The community is a grounding place where individuals can feed others and be nourished in return. When an individual does not have community, Somé (1999) explained, "you are not listened to; you don't have a place you can go to and feel that you really belong. You don't have people to affirm who you are and to support you in bringing forward your [practices]" (p. 65). Her expertise in communal living claims that the absence of a commune disempowers a person's psyche, "making the person vulnerable to consumerism and all the things that come along with it" (p. 65). Current schooling practices reflect a capitalist philosophy that promotes social Darwinism, highlighting purely individualistic endeavors (Bowles & Gintis, 1976), a practice diametrically opposed to Somé's experiences of group identity. Strictly individualistic efforts denigrate the importance of community. The absence of community "leaves many people who have wonderful [practices], wonderful contributions to make, hold back their [practices], not knowing where to put them" (Somé, 1999, p. 65). If one does not have a commune to share our practices, "we experience a blockage inside, and this blockage affects us spiritually, mentally, and physically in many different ways" (p. 65). El vivir comunitario includes a balanced existence of critical ancestral praxis that sustains a community that is not separate from the immediate environment. Without this community, "we are left without a home, a home to go to when we need to be seen" (p. 65). MEChA became a home where each individual student was recognized as someone who brought forth a practice that was nurtured by our collective flame of inspiration and commitment in a myriad of spatial commonplaces. They supported one another spiritually, emotionally, mentally, and physically in different ways and invited adults to participate in their world of practice, around a circle that kept an ancient fire alive.

That students successfully recruited others to participate in the organization beyond the booming school-wide assembly was a clear sign that they were interested in expanding their positive experiences with a shared *indigenismo*, or ancestral heritage, and learning about shared familial historical practices that crossed linguistic and sociological practices. Together, we felt pride in sharpening our historical awareness in a collective effort to journey through restrictive policies that strip away our integrity. Since its inception in 1969, MEChA was formed to build avenues for educational excellence *y el desarrollo de un rostro propio y un corazón puro* (Marin, 2009, February 27), an ancient practice that shapes our identity and molds our hearts as an act of resistance amidst a hostile political climate that pushes us to fit a Eurocentric standard of being.

Itzel took a leadership role in the organization of the second assembly of the year and accepted the group's challenge to emcee the program with Cynthia. Even though Itzel felt trepidation in speaking in front of a large crowd, she slowly took ownership of the microphone. She chose to relate to the audience like nobody else had that day. On one occasion, she got off the stage and walked toward the audience. The spotlight followed her as she engaged the audience with questions like: "Who can tell me why we are here today?", "What do you think about the assembly so far?", and "How about the music?" Itzel continued the spirit of student-leadership as she engaged with a larger, campus-wide audience. She included the audience as active participants of the goals of our gathering. This was a monumental point in Itzel's leadership. After this, she increasingly took more initiative in developing MEChA's goals throughout the 2009–2010 academic year.

Itzel and Dora bonded over their participation in MEChA. They increasingly spent more time with their familias outside of school hours. Dora's participation was key to establishing the visions of the group. Once she voiced her vision, others chimed in and shared their own ideas. Itzel had the idea of making flyers for our activities. She immediately took to designing them and printing them for dissemination. Her inkling to take care of the technological aspects of the organization earned her the name of "technology expert," one that adopted the responsibility of care-taking for digital tools that would help promote our organization. On one occasion, she passed out a flyer to an event at the Korean church down the street, "La Red de El Sereno," to her friend, an ECS student, and said, "You're *stewpid* if you don't come here." Using language play, Itzel shared her pride in her awareness and involvement of community events. "La Red de El Sereno" is a collaborative that promotes awareness about the extension of the 710 freeway through our neighborhood by the California Department of Transportation.

The spark that ignited the resurrection of a MEChA circle of student activists at Lomas High School was the participation of three sisters who were highly involved in Danza outside school grounds. Student inquiry is not restricted to the four walls of a classroom or school grounds. In fact, it is within these off-campus informal spaces that students co-constructed a positive ecology toward el vivir comunitario. Dora's older sister, Xochitl, had been dancing for three years prior to the re-seeding of MEChA on campus. Her devotion to carrying on the ancient practice of danzing spilled over to both of her sisters, Dora and Cynthia, who were nominated co-chairs of MEChA in 2009. It was their participation as a family unit of three sisters, in and outside school grounds, that magnetized the curiosity and practice of other students to participate in off-campus Danza sessions on weekday evenings at a local city park's recreational center in East Los Angeles. It was in this space that students cemented their connections to one another, with minimal adult intervention.

A Danza círculo is kept alive by the fire that connects the lit coal in the middle with the one burning inside, each individual danzing around the center. The coal usually burns *copalli*, tree resin, emanating white, slow-rising clouds of a strong-sweet-familiar scent of sacred space. The small fire burns in a ceramic piece that usually portrays an archaeological representation of indigenous iconography. Other items placed in the center grounds vary by *sahumadora*; they include pieces of dried food, mini-effigies, feathers, and clay figurines. These items carry a profound significance to the historical cultural practices that we have developed over time. *Estas reliquias* are sacred because we hold them with high esteem and they become part of the fabric that weave our *rostros* together.

Itzel tells of her initial resistance to join the Danza circle when she arrived at the community park for the first time: "I didn't want to take my shoes off on the street." She felt uncomfortable, but then she noticed families circling around the fire, young children included, dancing in sync to the rhythm of the ancient drum. "I thought I was too young to enter," she remembers. Danzing is a *cargo*,[2] and Itzel knew that. Aside from the physical demands of Danza (it is common to form foot blisters at the beginning), one enters the circle to connect with others as a community that ideally balances independent interdependence. The significance of having our bare feet touch the ground seals our connection to the land beneath our soles. Itzel was invited by her peers to join the circle, but she recalls her father as a presence that pulled her in: "I would feel um, like my dad would be proud of me." We were in my home when she shared her reflections about her participation in MEChA with me. She confided, "I would have a relationship with him [chokes up] back then not as much as I do now, um, I was very happy for myself that I was doing that [pauses] for him [pauses in tears]…."

I was invited to join in the Danza *círculo* on several occasions, and one evening I hesitantly accepted. It was a difficult step for me because I associated Danza with several unpleasant experiences, some conscious and others under my cognitive radar. You see, my maternal grandfather was a Danzante as an adolescent in the late 1930s and early 1940s while he lived in a small rancho outside Huejúcar, Jalisco. I remember hearing stories about his deep love of Danza, yet I resisted his memory because while he was an adult, his behavior inflicted deep pain within our family. So when I was exposed to Danza circles during my late teens, I resisted entering the practice. It was easy for me to attach myself to the negative commentary I heard about some Danza circles. It was not until students decided to start a Danza circle at Lomas that I became increasingly involved because, all of a sudden, I associated Danza practices with educational reform. Danzing to the beat of the ancient drum *on campus* localized the experienced to the learning (or not) that happened in between the walls of the classrooms, the lunch areas, the administrative offices and teacher's lounges, the football field and locked restrooms, the hallways and handball courts. It was as if we were waking up by stomping on the ground, in a circle with old time on our side.

So when Itzel's participation in Danza was described as a healing mechanism for her relationship to her father, the old fire awakened. A once warm and close relationship was slowly severed and turned distant after her parents divorced. Her father left her and her mother when she was young. During her visits after the divorce, she remembers his stories about Danza: "He had a *copilli*,[3] large and round. I've never seen it though," she regrets, "because it's in Mexico." She remembers telling him for the first time that she had taken up Danza, "Oh Dad, I'm doing Danza [pauses in tears] and he was like, 'oh really?'...And I was like, 'yeah,' and he was like, 'show me some steps [we both laugh] and he started danzing and um, we started danzing...together and he was making fun of me because I didn't know how to do it right." He did, however "ask my grandma to bring me his *chachayotes*.... I felt really honored." She stops and cries for a minute. I listen reverentially and cry too, for the deep connection we feel for the complex relationships with our family members. She wipes her tears from her face and continues, "And then he was showing me...his picture of when he was a Danzante. He has a whole album." Itzel's face lights up when she tells about the time her Dad took her to the *ensayo*, "He stayed to watch me [pauses with tears], and I was so happy! I was so happy he was there [cries], and I couldn't get the *pasos* right, but I stayed there for two whole years and I think I improved [by] sharing with everyone."

Turning to the larger story of the past contextualizes our present life circumstances and *humanizes* the characters in it. For example, Itzel instantly found a connection with her father when she saw him age in the context of the historicized relationship between Mexico and Spain and Mexico and the United States. Throughout this process, we were simultaneously *naming* the structures of power that have interacted within the coloniality of power over time. Humanizing our family members is not to say that we absolve individuals of their own responsibility to make informed decisions, but we must understand these circumstances as a dialectic, a Hegelian process that combines two antithetical arguments into a synthesized truth. These characters are products of a contested history. So for me, it has been a healing process to open up the possibilities of learning about my grandfather's life work of building houses by making bricks out of mud and cow manure, plowing the fields and enjoying his smoke, harmonica, and Danza. Going through the process of *historicizing* experiences through the eyes of my mother and grandmother humanizes my grandfather's memory and unravels the knots of pain our bodies have endured over time. While both Itzel and I initially resisted participation in Danza, we were encouraged by the group's strong standing, and we were nourished by their medicina, their remedios for ailments that are not just physical. Their presence sustained us while we experienced the initial discomfort of unearthing emotional pain. Ultimately, their support and our willingness to trust our community engaged us in a process of healing our pained histories through the figured world of Danza in MEChA.

Danza has the capacity to bring people together without the limitations of *just using* verbal language. Danza Azteca also uses body language and semiotics to connect danzantes with one another in a spiritual and historical approach. Itzel acknowledges the "unity" that she felt during her participation in Danza:

> [We] would always go together to any practice... at the Placita Olvera or any other place... and I love that...it's just very nice to be in a group... my first year in high school I didn't do anything and I felt so worthless. I felt like I was going to school for nothing because I wasn't involved in something I was passionate about.

Itzel shares Sobonfu Somé's feelings about community.

> Mario Aguilar (2009) pronounced Danza Azteca as
>   a complex membership that emphasizes unity with the ancestral traditions of México; conformity to the varied expressions of this ancestral heritage... and a way on which to walk in various "worlds" of experience: the day to day world of the profane and its parallel outlook onto the world of the sacred. (p. 544)

As a figured world, this particular Danza circle took to reviving Nahuatl[4] to non-Nahuatl speakers of Mesoamerican descent.

Participating in Danza reinforces the knowledge systems of our ancestors, as passed down from one generation to the next. Danza carries a positive outlook into the world from a position of resistance that has maintained a tradition alive despite the forces of colonial domination. Danza traditions can be traced back to the documented examples of the codices, and they have evolved over time. Sfard and Prusak (2005) contended that "telling identities," even if individually told, are a product of collective storytelling in which these stories are "constantly created and re-created in interactions between people" (p. 15). Continued interactions between people are vital ingredients for community building. Somé (1999) recognized that the goal of a community is to incorporate each member as a stand-alone contributor to the whole so that the individual is given an opportunity to share his/her practices. Each member contributes their practice, or else the community dies, leaving people without a home where they are recognized. I have often heard that there is no "i" in team. Yet it takes skill to balance independent interdependence, for a strong community is comprised of dedicated individuals. The community becomes a matrix of multidimensional aspects of temporal, spatial, and social commonplaces. These communities, socially figured, sustain themselves through visceral and explicit dialogue and practice (Wenger, 2010).

Danza, a figured world that promotes cultural awareness, one of the foundations of MEChA, became the centripetal force that thrust a spiral of continued interactions around political, social, psychological, and spiritual meaning making within the community. MEChA's core members organized bi-weekly meetings in addition to workshops, field trips, and collaborations with other participants. MEChA was the space in which students contributed their individual practices for the benefit of a collective. And these practices fed each other in a larger context, spilling into each individual's daily activities, even outside of the collective MEChA space. Itzel's participation in MEChA was a stark difference from her involvement in ROTC[5] during the first two years of high school. It is useful to describe Itzel's perceived differences between both organizations to get a glimpse of the meaning she places on one over the other.

Itzel was part of ROTC, "the army thing," during her first two years of high school. She joined because she wanted "to be in something." She was itching to "give my time and dedicate myself into something but I didn't know what so that's what I chose." Although she felt part of a community of practice in the established ROTC program and "had a good time attending parades and stuff," she "really wasn't motivated to be there." Itzel was a core member of MEChA during her last two years of high school, and this experience was a great contrast: "I think being part of something that you're passionate about for me was MEChA, [it] is worth my time because when I was in ROTC I was like oh this was a waste of time." Her involvement with MEChA evoked a different feeling: "I wanted to be there, I felt that I wasn't doing it just for anything. I was doing it for a reason even though I didn't know what it was...

it's not something you're doing because you're bored because I don't think anyone's bored." Itzel pointed to increased interest in making MEChA her home, one that mirrored her family experiences and history. Somé (1999) shared that a community comes together for a specific purpose, and each player in the community contributes their unique practice. Itzel did not resonate with the purpose of "the army thing." She gravitated toward MEChA, which invoked her family history and helped form her ancestral identity. Itzel says, "we need to place our effort and our time into something we're really passionate about and you get the feeling back just to see something grow even though you don't know what it is…you feel good about yourself… it's not something you take for granted."

> *"Cuando apuntamos el dedo, tres nos regresan a nosotros."*
> 'When we point a finger, three are pointing back at us.'—*Abuelitas*

This common saying in Spanish refers to the practice of looking at oneself as a responsible player in the game of life. During one of our health-conscious community meetings in Boyle Heights with Proyecto Jardín, a male elder scolded a young mother for letting her child play with a cell phone on her lap. The explanation given to the group was that cell phones carry dangerous frequencies that developing children should not be exposed to at such a young age. As a responsible mother, he supposed, she would protect her child from harm. His perception placed blame on the young mother, asserting that her "irresponsible way of parenting" needed to change. A young female from across the room immediately shot up from her seat and pointed her finger into the air: "Dice mi abuelita que cuando apuntamos el dedo, tres nos regresan a nosotros." I instantly remembered my grandmother's words. Verbatim.

When we point a judgmental finger at another, there are three pointing at us, a reminder that we, too, play an important role in the shaping of life's circumstances. Given a space to unfold their understanding of the world, MEChA students show us by example that it is our responsibility to work within ourselves, as well as to bridge relationships with others to find solutions to the problems we see through the teachings of our abuelitas. The practice of inner reflection, coupled with critical consciousness of societal expressions, spawns our work as activistas (Moreno Sandoval et al., 2016). When we challenge linguistic and social repertoires, we must consider our own positionalities within the historical context in which we live. We are to assume responsibility for our actions, outside the common practice of *just* blaming others for societies' mishaps, stripping us away from our own agency. The male elder stopped dead in his tracks, remained silent, y le dió razón a la muchacha. He stopped his blaming, and we continued our dialogue around health consciousness within the Eastside of Los Angeles. We continued to interact with him through Lomas High School's Centro de Padres (more details about intersections with el Centro de Padres will be offered in Chapter 6).

Young people who have participated in our circles have demonstrated a keen awareness of critical self-reflection that lays out an example for adults to follow. Their practices may be traced to the reawakening of old practices, which brought seemingly unrelated people together. Their leadership socially (re)constructed a figured world of the familiar ways of our familias.

But what happens when collective identity forming evolves behind the curtain of self-hatred? When high school students who are vulnerable to a combined systems of power that maintain a monolingual, standard nationalism within a European-centered heritage, students are forced to divorce themselves from their ancestral praxis, becoming open to consumerism and an inferior sense of self/community, as Sobonfu Somé (2000) has reminded us. There is no community sanctioned by the institutions that promote social capital to sustain the practices that young people bring around their fire. Yet there are pockets of cultural spaces and symbologies that feed a common world of ancestral praxis everywhere; we just have to pay attention to the underlying symbols and behavior that can be traced across time.

4.2   INTERNALIZED COLONIZATION UNEARTHED, PLANTING A COLLECTIVE CRITICAL CONSCIOUSNESS

"Hay que empezar con nuestro aplauso, ready? ¡ce-ome-yei-nahui!" After everyone in the circle introduced ourselves, Dora welcomed everyone to our community workshop at the Eastside Café in March 2010, entitled *What is Mesoamerica?* Those of us who were familiar with the unity clap began to put our palms together. Over time, our sound waves synchronized to emanate one single clap with a loud vibration that could probably be heard at the top of Lomas High School, a mile away. Community members who were present who had not yet attended one of our meetings could easily clap with us. We learned this clap from as far back as the Civil Rights Movement, from our brothers and sisters in the struggle who continue to fight for justice. Thirteen of us came together on that day: five high school students, three single male adult community members (Lomas High School 1980 and 2010 alumni), one eight-year-old male and his father, and two educators. During our introductions, there was one adult male, José, who was more comfortable speaking in Spanish. There was an attempt to speak in Spanish for the next few minutes, with some struggle. Soon we reverted back to English, making sure along the way that José could express himself in Spanish and understand what we were saying with a translator sitting next to him.

"Who knows why we're here today?" Dora asks. We agreed that we were coming together to learn about our ancestral heritage, yet some questions lingered: What is Mesoamerica? What does Lomas have to offer? How can youth across El Sereno campuses engage in dialogue and action? What do youth need from adults? What is happening with the planned extension of the 710 FWY cutting through our neighborhood? Both sisters pointed to the agenda the youngest one had written on the board and reminded us why the workshop had been organized in the first place. The 4084 minutes of documented meetings over eight and a half months all began with students' initiative to write the agenda on the board, begin the meetings with the unity clap and dialogue, questioning and exploring solutions. Table 4.2 illustrates the variety of meetings that were held and a sample of the reasons that students called us to gather.

Our gatherings were directed by both sisters, Dora and Cynthia, who took the initiative to answer questions that came up during the workshops, one of which was: "What are we going to do about the proposed extension of the 710 FWY through our neighborhood?" While students did not have simple solutions, we opened up dialogue about the potential of our collective voice, our general well-being, self-identity, and visions about how we were to build our future. Particular attention was given to health issues related to respiration and food consumption. The next part of the meeting was directed Mr. Dueñas, Mexican American studies professor at Lomas High School. He was to facilitate a workshop on re-discovering our own positionalities, our historical knowledge systems that could give us insight into the difficult questions we posed.

"So what is being indigenous anyway?" Mr. Dueñas asked. A few minutes before our start time, he set up the space to make it more conducive to dialogue. He laid out a collection of *reliquias*, ranging from wooden

Table 4.2   MEChA Documented Gatherings, 2010

Dates	Varied purposes	Total mins.	File types	Locations
14 January 2010– 2 October 2010	Define MEChA/ Mesoamerica/ Indigenous	4084.97	Audio	Lomas High School classrooms/ outdoors/ Multipurpose room
	Carry out school assemblies/body gatherings/garden		Movies	Homes
	Dialogue food practices		Images	Ascot Hills
	Collaborate with transdisciplinary teachers, Centro de Padres, and community members		Documents	Community cultural spaces
	Reflections		(409 files total)	Car rides

carved masks, pottery, clay figurines, and vessels to a slew of books on *indigenismo* and some personal sacred items. On the opposite side of the space, there were three pieces of butcher paper, human-size length, with the questions, "What is indigenous?" and "¿Qué es indígena?" on all three sheets. In the middle of the room, a white screen projected a map of Mesoamerica with a set of dates that delimited various periods of the 3500 years of documented history. We slowly trickled into the space, absorbing the old smell of *copal*, and sat in a circle on different colored chairs. The cement floors kept the space cool from the warm sun as it began to feed the first sprouts of spring.

The topic that ensued weighed heavily on our hearts. We talked about the shame within our society associated with even referring to the "indio" side of our heritage, as it is often felt to be "uncivilized." We spoke of the times our families have perpetuated this hierarchy of being by using terms like: "patas rajadas," "incivilizados," "burros," "os pa' nada," "prietos," "not smart," "backwards thinking," etc., to refer to our native ancestry. For example, one student spoke of a time when a little cousin was born, and the family was quick to ask what color skin and eyes he wore. It was understood that lighter shades were better.

Of course, there are also tricks or home remedies one can apply to maintain a light tone, or forge one if it wasn't already present. What message does this practice give to our collective image? If we are to glorify light skin and light eyes, how does that possibly place our mixed ancestral makeup outside of the racist practices of referring to phenotypic characteristics within judgmental perceptions? And how do these internally colonizing practices spill over into our approaches to knowledge (re)production? If our indigenous phenotype is less favorable, does our intellectual and creative merit as indigenous people have value in our society? The colonial practice of differentiating people based on phenotypic characteristics continues to pervade our society today (Omi & Winant, 1994). Our collective questioned these practices by peeking into our precedential form of identification of people during pre-colonial times.

We collectively reflected on our shared ancestral heritage of the US Southwest, Mexico, El Salvador, and Guatemala. Both sisters led a discussion about the uncovering of our historical experiences as a shared discourse that unites us in subversive ways. "It's important for people to know their history," Cynthia says. "We're learning all from each other and we're building up." The remainder of the two-and-a-half-hour session focused on naming the shame that we have been conditioned to feel as mestizos, glorifying our European heritage and feeling shame for our indigenous history. We named this a colonizing practice that has maintained us silenced for so long and we silently cried for the chipping away of our dignity. Yet this depth of intimacy brought about a sense of closeness, the very practice of decolonizing our identities by uncovering our cultural wealth, which nonetheless remains vibrant in our families' stories and practices. We connected the dots between old codices and Danza practices. We armed ourselves with pride in our shared history as descendants of native peoples on this hemisphere while still maintaining a dialectic, bringing into question the common approach of romanticizing the past as a utopian delicacy. We learned about our history within a contested space that tells the evolutionary story of humanity at its best and at its worst.

Mr. Ambrocio, teacher and MEChA supporter, explains the way in which we have been conditioned to think over time: "Imagine an onion and all of its layers." He makes a fist in front of his chest and looks at it. With his other hand, he covers up his fist. He explains that we are like an onion with intricate layers of historical experiences. He tells about the layers that grew on us as native peoples of this hemisphere upon the arrival and influence of Spanish conquistadors. He points out that their presence began to change the way we perceive ourselves in comparison to them because, for the first time, we experienced the beginnings of cultural genocide. Already vulnerable to foreign forces because of internal conflict, indigenous peoples' dignity began to chip away with the dominant force of European righteousness.

"Now imagine," Mr. Ambrocio continues with something like, "if that onion layer grew another one; this time of English and U.S. Imperialism." He pushes us to think of language as an example of this layering of the onion that is us. "In some cases, we've lost our original languages." He pauses for a moment, hands now open in front of him, shaking. There is a long silence in the room. We all pondered this for a while. I remember feeling the fibers of my muscles tense, feeling the heavy layers that we carry on our backs. Circling up around dialogue that raised our consciousness about our positionalities in the world did not drop us into victimization mode, which often leads us to passive characters, waiting for superman to save us. Instead, we braced ourselves and took charge of continuing a slow-burning fire, from the deepest core of our existence, for ourselves, for our families, for our earth.

Our living ancestral praxis means that we become curious about multiple tellings of stories, especially when we compare this "informal" learning to the "formal" learning of our history books. We became more aware of how language, as a mediating tool, reinforces a process of an understanding of the world. People often ask, "What is the whole point of learning about your history anyway? Why would we characterize learning about our history as important?" I asked our group the same question. Here is a paraphrase of Josué's response:

> The whole point to learning about ourselves is not just for ourselves. We learn about ourselves to deepen our roots, connect with our families. And then to relate to others. We have more in common than differences. What can we share with others if we are not sure of who we are?

By uncovering the layers, learning how to think critically for ourselves, and incorporating the knowledge that our ancestral history illustrates, we slowly increased our insight, moving together, hand-in-hand, in a circular motion, dancing to one heartbeat. We gained strength from making sense of our positionalities together. We also learned to extend compassion to ourselves, for we, too, have been conditioned to accumulate and spit out venom to ourselves and to each other. We learned to look at ourselves as powerful agents of decolonizing individuals within our own thought patterns and actions, for example, by connecting our consciousness to our bodies as the decolonizing flesh.

Elmer, Itzel, and Cynthia, juniors and core members of MEChA, attended a Raza Conference at UCLA and reported what they had learned at our "What is indigenous?" workshop at the Eastside Café the next day. Elmer tells us what he learned about the educational budget cuts that are affecting teachers, students, and school spaces. He shares the knowledge that he and two other MEChISTAS gained when attending a Raza Youth Conference at UCLA the day prior to our workshop: "I really liked X-ray. They told us to pick three [body] parts of what was most important to us...I chose my eyes, my heart, and hands...because eyes say a lot about different people. My heart feels everything and you need your hands for everything." When our bodies are explicitly incorporated as part of our associations with learning, students may ground their contributions with themselves, as bodies that think, feel, and see. Elmer continues, "and [when] we gathered around, everyone else had the same thing: eyes, heart, hands, and stuff...no matter how far we live [from each other],...[we are] going through the same problem. What can we do to help each other out?" Elmer is pointing to a larger concept of imagined community.

The students who attended the conference pushed us to think about an imagined community that connects individuals despite our physical presence. It rests on the collective consciousness of the *nepantla* of our bodies, connected to the earth, the physical topography that feeds us, a social commonplace that holds the figured world of contextual interactions. We came together to celebrate our bodies connected to a physical space that sustains us. After all, we exchange gases with the earth and our physical human structure contains similar compounds. Mr. Dueñas reminded us that our original calendar system is based on a 20–13 count system, which may be connected to the physical representations of our bodies. We have twenty phalanges and thirteen joints. Our knowledge systems are intimately connected to the physical spaces of flesh and earth. This is not a common way of knowing in schools. Instead, our original knowledge systems that have inhabited this hemisphere for millennia are seen as backwards and inferior in the hierarchy of knowledge systems.

To resist a common discourse of deficit notions of our epistemic knowledge, we became increasingly proud to wear our cultural heritage on our sleeves, in our discourse, and among our families and friends. We adopted a common language as we learned more about Mesoamerican history during our workshops at the Los Angeles County Museum of Art (LACMA) and at our campus when LACMA Mesoamerican educator Tocatzin would come to Lomas High School and our community spaces like Eastside Café and Xocolatl to facilitate our learning about Mesoamerica. Students organized activities outside instructional hours, within and beyond the high school campus, in our neighborhood and in our homes. Some of the activities organized include Danza, school assemblies, body planning meetings, mesa meetings,[6] workshops, social gatherings, visits to museums, community events, and reflection time. It was in these informal spaces that students were able to co-construct a practice that drew upon the cultural wealth of the community, while questioning the systems of power that perpetuate a negative image of ourselves and our families. Table 4.3 shows the ways in which students and adults developed inquiry and action as collaborators.

Students were in charge of scheduling and facilitating our gatherings. The majority of initiative came from both sisters, Dora and Cynthia, as nominated co-chairs of the organization. For example, on one occasion, Dora suggested that our meetings be held more regularly and closer to campus for increased access to other students. Also, students collaborated

Table 4.3 Student inquiry and adult-situated action within a student-led organization

Student inquiry and action	Adult inquiry and action
• Co-construct agendas	• Act as a resource
• Practice curiosity	• Advocate youth voice and action to stakeholders
• Freedom of expression	• Question systems of power
• Schedule and cancel meetings at will	• Co-construct ideas
• Develop creativity	• Ask students for permission
• Begin each meeting	• Freedom of expression
• Extend social networks	• Active listening
• Use digital media	• Establish an integral approach
• Active listening	• Engage in critical reflection
• Maintain integrity	
• Engage in critical reflection	

on the themes to be presented at the school-wide assemblies and met on their own (oftentimes without an adult) to practice the presentation or to go over certain club responsibilities. This demonstrated students' ownership of the activities that sprouted from their initial curiosities.

In December 2009, after stating the three goals that they had come up with prior to our meeting, Mr. Floragon asked me if I would consider sponsoring MEChA. I was honored that he would ask me to participate, and I jumped at the opportunity to work with students in an informal setting. Promoting cultural awareness, advancing college-going rates, and connecting to the community are passions for me. Since I had moved back to El Sereno, it seemed like the perfect fit. A week later, I met a group of students at Xocolatl.

The students told me, "I remember when we first met you, you were so nice, Cueponcaxochitl, but we couldn't even say your name. It took us a while to get it because we never even heard of it before." Students welcomed my presence and secretly asked each other about me before our formal introductions. Itzel wasn't present at our first meeting, but I did hear two things about her: (1) her mom had taken her cell phone away because she was caught lying to her about a party, and (2) she was suspended for smoking in a school bathroom.

I met Itzel the weekend of our first mesa meeting[7] at Xocolatl. I introduced myself as a Xicana graduate student at UCLA, and as a family member and resident of El Sereno. I spent most of the meeting listening. I soon realized that what was happening in MEChA was a story of subversive resistance from the bottom up, without the restrictions of subtractive schooling practices. At the same time, I was a participant observer in the *Exploring Computer Science* class on campus. I did not realize, however, that my position in both worlds would somehow bridge these two seemingly opposite disciplines.

As activists, Mr. Dueñas and Mr. Floragon were also cultural proponents in college. Since there wasn't much formal room on campus for free exploration of our cultural history, they welcomed the opportunity to continue their involvement in MEChA as high school educators. At that time, the three of us lived within a six-mile radius. Our collective efforts as adults helped to open up a space for students to speak, create spaces for dialogue and inquiry, and activism. Through our involvement, we learned that our role as adults was to hold up a mirror to students so that they would have the opportunity to pay attention to themselves, their families, and our shared community. This allowed students to spawn dialogue and action about something that was important and meaningful to them. By mere living spaces, it was connected to our common vision as adults.

One example of this facilitation sprouted from our first collective meeting at Xocolatl in January 2010. Upon discussing the details of operationalizing our goals, Dora said, "I want us to go to Skid Row and feed the homeless people." When Dora mentioned that she wanted "us to go to Skid Row," a run-down area in Downtown Los Angeles, "and feed the homeless people," we thought that we would reflect on that statement for a bit. My field notes for that day read: "Although we did not achieve a consensus to literally walk to Skid Row, we turned the mirror back onto our community and its relationship with food." Eating became an area of interest among students, as well as one topic (of several) that Mr. Floragon and his students had developed in their class on Leadership Development in Interethnic Studies (LDIR) using Youth Participatory Action Research. Alberto, an LDIR student and MEChA member, was proud to bring up the insight he was learning in class. Another topic in the LDIR class was paying attention to green space in the community.

Alberto invited us to a community presentation his LDIR class was giving the next day about "having more urban green space in the community." He told us that green space "makes it look better" and gave the example of "having a park." He feared that if there weren't enough parks in a community, people's health might decrease and they might slip into "drugs and stuff like that." He pushed us to think about parks as a space that promoted healthy practices. All the while, Mr. Floragon sat beside him, silent. My field notes' written memory states:

> He just sat there, still, looking at his students with pride. When Alberto turned to him for direction, Mr. Floragon used his body language to indicate that Alberto knew what to say at times and on another time, he prodded a question that would help Alberto think about it.

In this way, there was a clear sense of ownership of their own learning. As adults, we would often spot them if they looked to us for help and push them to carry as much as they could with support. In this way, we encourage them to reach their Zones of Proximal Development (Vygotsky, 1978), a level at which students are just in between what they have already demonstrated that they are able to do on their own and new territory of development.

Dora and Itzel interject a reminder about Danza practice and unity around food, "How about we get people [to] experience Danza. It's on Lorena. The doors are always open. We should bring this up next meeting." Itzel backs up her call,

> Something I like a lot [about Danza] is that they share food. Not because I want to eat, but because I think it's a nice gesture to bring something for everyone...*siempre* hay leftovers *no hay* for half, or for a couple, you know?

Other students nod their heads in agreement, and one student jots it down on the agenda to be written on the whiteboard of the body meeting the next day. Soon our focus is to be shifted to chicahualistli (life force), or food.

After Alberto's invitation, Mr. Floragon checks a few last reminders: "By the next time we meet, think about what other ideas you have and how we can support you." Students shuffle papers and speak among themselves through body language and whispers. "There's a lot of things happening," Mr. Floragon continues, despite the multiple conversations,

> We're all working hard. Take care of yourselves. Finals week is next week. If you're not sure where you are in the class, talk to your teachers. I'm telling you from a teacher's perspective. Find out how you're doing in your classes.

More conversations are heard. He continues, "We want you to be getting good grades and be an example and model for other students." We were trained in the skill of multi-tasking, operating in various activities at the same time, with the common understanding of multiple centers, depending on where the louder voice sat at any given moment. It is Dora's birthday the next day. "What are you going to do for your birthday?" Alberto asks. "Go to your presentation!" Dora says in a loud voice, drowning out the noise of the rest of the crowd for a still moment, followed by a unifying, "Aaawww!"

Alberto continues, inspired, after feeling supported by the group, "One thing I told Armenta is that I'm thankful for being in that class because it actually opened my eyes to...things I didn't see before." He shares that "even when the class ends, I'm still going to do the green space, checking out the parks in other communities." These instances illustrate a semi-structured organization that makes room for students to speak up when they may not have otherwise. As adults, we must sustain the silent moments, even if they seem uncomfortable. Students need time to think and gather courage to become comfortable speaking.

Later, Mr. Floragon shared at one of our adult meetings, "You're following those questions in our meetings, I'm really proud of those students. They're really interested in creating that change."

I waited until the end of the meeting, just a few moments before we were to stand up and leave to go home, then I said, "I have a closing comment." I began to read from a paper I had in front of me on Sobonfu Somé's (2000) words on community, some of which I have cited earlier in this book:

> Community is the spirit, the guiding light of the tribe, whereby people come together in order to fulfill a specific purpose, to help others fulfill their purpose, and to take care of one another. The goal of the community is to make sure that each member of the community is heard and is properly giving the [practices] that they have brought to this world. Without these [practices], the community dies. And without the community, the individual is left without a place where they can contribute. And so the community is that grounding place where people come and share their [practices] and receive from others. When you don't have community, you are not listened to: you don't have a place you can go to and feel that you really belong. You don't have people to affirm who you are and to support you in bringing forward your [practices]. What this does to the person's psyche is that it disempowers it, making the person vulnerable to consumerism and all the things that come along with it. Also, it leaves many people who have wonderful [practices], wonderful contributions to make, hold back their [practices], not knowing where to put them. And without the unloading of our [practices] we experience a blockage inside, and this blockage affects us spiritually, mentally, and physically in many different ways. We are left without a home, a home to go to when we need to be seen. (pp. 22–23)

Our gatherings became a space for open dialogue that promoted communal health consciousness. Each of us carried a torch that was needed for the molding of a movement that cultivated a positive learning ecology. We did not feel the hostility or time pressure as much as we did in the bell-driven pacing of time on campus. Even if we held meetings after school, the stale paint on the walls and the intercom, as well as the pressure teachers felt to finish their attendance registers and grades at the

end of each term, interrupted our creativity. We spent most of our planning activities off campus and continued our activism on campus during
school lunchtime, after school, and in class time in two school assemblies
during the year.

Another aspect of MEChA organizing was the support that students
offered to one another. At every mesa meeting, there was an element of
taking turns writing the agenda on the board (Fig. 4.1).

These included the items that we needed to address at the meeting,
who was responsible for bringing it up, and tag team responsibilities. We
were to hold each other accountable for thinking and acting together to
meet our collective vision to: (a) promote cultural awareness, (b) advance
college-going opportunities, and (c) connect to the community. In this
context, community signified spaces that were connected to and outside
the high school campus. We practiced a sense of unity, even in ritual as
a part of our gatherings. For example, students commonly began our
meetings with the unity clap. These routines became part of a socially

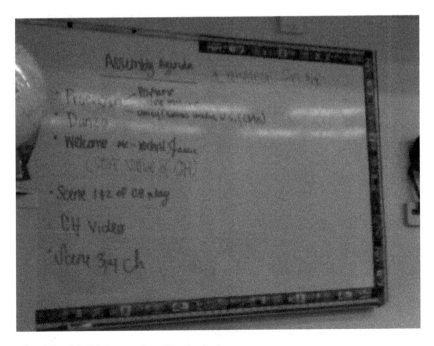

Fig. 4.1   MEChA agenda at Barrio Action

constructed world that enlisted our voluntary membership. These movements registered as a thread that connected us to activism in the United States previously led by Xican@ peoples who have worked collectively toward dignity and educational excellence in our communities. Just as it is important to allow our efforts to spill over into the larger community of the high school campus within another temporal and spatial context, I advocate schools as the central force of a community.

As a team, we took that preliminary idea of food and poverty and connected it to the content we were learning in some of our classes. For example, Alberto was enrolled in Mr. Floragon's LDIR class, and Dora was part of the Mexican American Studies class. Both classes were represented by a student and a teacher. The rest of the students were interlaced between the on-campus organizations United Students and Latinas Unidas, both of which are connected to a non-profit, Inner City Struggle. In addition, Latinas Unidas is a campus club sponsored by another teacher. I will address this and collaboration among teachers more in Chapter 6, but for now, I will briefly describe the simultaneity of our collective actions. For one, students were motivated to meet after school hours in informal spaces within the community—McDonald's, Barrio Action, Eastside Café, Xocolatl, and our homes. Each space offered a reminder of our connections with the community. While I cringed at the idea of meeting at McDonald's when some students suggested it, I realized that we needed to be flexible, not militant, about our meeting space. Besides, we had trouble finding another space to meet at that hour that was easily accessible to students. Few purchases were made, and when they were, nobody looked down upon it. Some students decided to open up a dialogue about it. Once, we asked the staff to turn the music down. We also practiced singing to "Ella's Song" by Sweet Honey in the Rock, while clapping our hands.[8] Another time, we took over six tables to make jewelry for a fundraising event. JA! So it became a space where we challenged the monopolizing food industry that the McDonald's corporation represents by appropriating it to fit our needs. We met there most Tuesday nights when Xocolatl was not available, just before the general body meetings on Wednesdays at lunchtime on campus.

We, MEChA, stand as a collective who seeks to build a positive learning environment that acknowledges the historical knowledge systems of our families who have inhabited the Western hemisphere for millennia. As such, for a moment, we seek to address those who suspect that cultural studies promote "the overthrow of the US government" or "resentment toward a race or class of people," as voters in Arizona did in their justification of banning Mexican American Studies. We need to make something as clear as water here: While developing a critical consciousness about the socio-historical realities that directly relate to our families and, by extension, communities, we become aware of *systems of power* that have privileged European knowledge. As such, we command respect for a *multiplicity of knowledge systems* (Paris, 2012) as equally valued through grassroots approaches to educational excellence that reflect locally situated action (Vaughan, 2002). This is not meant to feed another hierarchy of knowledge systems, but to level out the playing field with multiple ways of living and learning.

4.3   DRAWING ON OUR FAMILIAS TO BRING IT BACK HOME

As our focus on communal health practices increased during our meetings with students, we began to see family members trickle into our dialogues. Parents saw a connection to their own histories as valued practices that we were interested in learning more about. For example, the Parent Center on campus welcomed students during lunch, particularly Dora and Itzel, who had established a relationship with them by popping into the center between classes or during lunch. They often had food available that was *not* the school lunch. The Parent Center included the participation of several parents who were interested in preserving ancestral praxis as well. The center hosted "El Trueque" (an event that promoted trading items of economic value), sunrise gatherings around a fire, and healthy food promotion workshops that re-introduced original foods like nopales, chile, frijoles, hand-made tortillas, calabazitas, etc.

On one occasion, the MEChA "family of five" (Dora, Cynthia, Xochitl, Carolina, and Junior) and I attended a community workshop sponsored by Mujeres de Maíz on ancestral foodways, offered by Claudia Serrato. We learned about different foods that we weren't as aware of, such as chia, amaranto, quinoa, verdolagas, epazote, papalotl, etc. This brought us closer to our families, but at the same time, some of us had a hard time because we tend to get so defensive about our foods. For example, Xochitl tells of her first encounters with healthy eating, "Ugh, me caía tan gorda because I couldn't stand all that healthy stuff she was eating. I loved my fried stuff." But we slowly learned how to politicize our foods, and we are still learning. Itzel's mom told us about "all of my family members slowly dying off to diseases like heart disease and diabetes." She told us that she quickly had to figure out how to spare herself from what she perceived as death's tapping call.

On another occasion, one MEChA father shared his knowledge about growing corn in Oaxaca: "Hay milpa de riego y milpa de lluvia." He shared stories about his connections with the land, sembrando frijol, maíz, calabaza y trigo. Tocatzin tailored his workshops to our increased connections with the land in our Mesoamerican Studies workshops on and off campus. Some parent volunteers from the Parent Center became regular attendees of MEChA-sponsored workshops. Dora and Cynthia invited their grandmother to sing a few songs at our last school assembly of the year. They were so proud to share that space with their grandmother, and she was honored to be recognized by young teens. Our connections to family involved deeper ties, which were spiritual, emotional, and carnal, which moved us toward un vivir comunitario.

There were instances when students came to our gatherings with heavy hearts. On one of those occasions, we explored the feeling of anger as it related to their developing critical consciousness. One male student shares, "When I feel anger, [I just] hold it in. It's just too much. You just explode." A female student responds to his comment, backing up his statement with another point about learning, "And how are we supposed to know what to do with [anger?] You don't go to classes where they say don't talk back or don't say these words... the whole communication thing is really difficult." While students did not specify what prompted their anger, anger came up spontaneously one day in which we had planned to discuss our pilot research study on collecting data on food and drink practices with mobile technology.

On this warm summer evening in El Sereno, we gathered at Xocolatl after students had returned from their respective summer day activities that included Fuerza training, UCLA CENS High School Scholars Program, Boys and Girls Club, Upward Bound, and a conference sponsored by the UCLA School of Public Health on the air quality of Boyle Heights, our neighboring community. It was customary for students to take turns sharing about what they learned in class. In fact, they were expected to be our eyes and ears while in these organizations, so they would normally take notes to prepare themselves to share the information with us. We learned about participatory sensing, the air quality of our extended neighborhood, and the political state of education today. Dora's brother, sister, and mother were present, as well as other students who had come to visit for the first time. There was a sharp exchange between Dora and her mom. The dialogue soon began to address some of the anger felt in the room after we had heard about the historic injustices in our neighborhoods in terms of health and education. We examined how these issues may influence our home situations.

Students surmised the space to be one of free rein for their direction. Within our small community of trusted individuals who brought our interests and developed thinking to the table, we became mirrors for each other. We helped each other see ourselves as active participants in our life's journey, as well as products of a colonial power that permeates our top-down policies in society, affecting our health and education. When Elisa saw her colega and her mom have an exchange that evoked a familiar feeling in her, she spoke. She talked about her way of coping with her anger toward her parents at times by writing them a letter, while struggling whether her parents would be willing to take a letter, as "I want them to hear it." Jason chimes in, "I put my headphones, ...and go for a long walk...I play guitar...[and] write lyrics down." Itzel shares that she holds in her anger and then she (snaps her fingers) responds harshly to someone else who had nothing to do with her source of anger in the first place. Xochitl offers her a suggestion, "Once you let it out, you can breathe again."

Learning happens best through self-discovery within ecologies that are non-threatening. When our affective filters are lowered, and we can express ourselves freely, knowing that we will not be judged. Here, magic happens. Students' confidence in assuming responsibility for their learning and practices for the betterment of our families and communities becomes a purpose that is worth all the time and energy that is invested. Emotional intelligence is key to the process of living and learning. It is through critical self-reflection that we can make sense of our pained histories and open the way toward accessing our full human capacity to think, feel, and act.

After most had shared their experiences with anger, Ivan spoke out, digesting what others had said and challenging the need to "let it out." Ivan shared some deep reflections about his emotions, including his fears of hurting others. "What hurts me the most is you can't let it out... You're angry at yourself, but you just don't know why. You don't know the answer to that. You don't know the solution to your own problem." He said that he does not have time to "sit in my bed [to] reflect. I don't write. I don't hear music, none of that...I mean those are wonderful things but for me it's always *pain*."

He mourns over not providing the best example for his younger brother who "likes" Ivan more than anyone in the family and wants to grow up to be "just like me." As a young male growing up in a complex world of gender expectations, Ivan finds himself "upset...knowing that you're just sick of yourself, knowing that you make mistakes yet everybody tries to influence you to do something that you don't want to." He reflects on the possible reasons behind his anger, not knowing where to turn: "you don't know what's wrong. That's what upsets me the most." His discourse continued with half-breaths while the rest of us actively listened.

Ivan added more flame to the fire of emotional anger and pain. We all sat silently, some of us wiping tears away from our faces. Although Ivan had visited the all-too-common self-blame for our society's ills, without a historical analysis, he had also practiced looking at himself as an agent in his reality. And he was desperately searching for answers. In a sense, Ivan felt the frustration that we inherit when our families have been exposed to the coloniality of power that perpetuates the historical abuse of our dignity. For example, most of us are either immigrants or descendants of immigrants. Since NAFTA, which was supposed to increase employment opportunities in foreign countries, the reality is that most families were *forced* to find economic opportunities elsewhere, such as in the backyards of the homes that created NAFTA in the first place. Since many of our families, as indigenous peoples displaced to an urban context, a hostile environment operated by racial projects (Omi & Winant, 1994), we *feel the pain*, yet sometimes we cannot name it. Ivan and the other students spoke loudly to the emotional experiences that interrupted their positive senses of self. Without a community to *make sense* of these experiences for collective action toward el vivir comunitario, we are often left without a home when we need to be seen. Students came together to support one another in their quest to support one another through their sadness and anger for justice in our communities.

Xochitl finally took the palabra after a long silence: "I want to thank you, Ivan, for sharing that with us, being comfortable enough... I really respect that. Thank you." Another male supported Ivan by asking, "Can I give a word of advice?" He recognized Ivan for sharing with the rest of us as well, and then talked about his experience in relation to Ivan's. He ended by referring back to the idea of finding positive approaches to coping with our emotions.

Our families may also suffer from emotional turmoil as a reflection of unequal childhoods. The coloniality of power has stripped our families apart based on racial projects (Lareau, 2003; Olmeca, 2009; Omi & Winant, 1994), such as unjust immigration policies that force some family members to cross the border without the impossible permission from the US government, for example. Still, students make sense of their emotional development together, provide support for one another, and begin to critically historicize their experiences through a socio-cultural lens that is critical of colonial forces. This does not mean that a superficial enactment of what is mistakenly perceived as evidence of internal transformation for enactment's sake, just to say that "I did it!" No. Action without internal transformation is meaningless. I am telling a collective story about recognizing a historical cultural essence that exists in and outside the colonial legacy that has been imposed upon us. It is up to us to liberate our oppressors (Freire, 1970), for once we reach a critical consciousness, it behooves us to unearth those tenants that may help us, our families, and our communities to reach el vivir comunitario.

After some more dialogue on the possible connections between larger, macro-issues and our experiences at home as Mesoamerican-descent peoples who have been vulnerable to colonialism, we understood the great need to mobilize consciousness in ourselves and our communities. We followed up with the original purpose of the meeting, which was to review the process of data collection, making connections to the foods we consume as a story that fits within the larger history of our families' dignity.

Though we are usually not trained psychologists, educators are constantly faced with situations that are emotionally difficult to process with our students, as well as within ourselves. Within the common structure of schooling, we do not have the proper systems in place that would hold a sacred space for students to comfortably process and grow from their experiences. Students teach me that while educational reform is complex, it must draw attention to home culture—first as a center that draws upon historical intellectual traditions, and second as a social commonplace to apply the extended learning experiences in schools. For example, in Mesoamerican times, los Guerreros de la Muerte Florecida (Marin, 2008) were/are characterized as one of the most difficult tasks for humankind to master: "la lucha más difícil que un ser humano pueda librar: la batalla interior para controlar el ego y así, muriendo al mundo material, hacer florecer el espíritu" (Marin, 2008, Web log message).

When one is conditioned to be individualistic within a consumerist capitalist society, one can lose track of the sense of community or the drive to self-less acts that benefit the whole rather than the immediacy of individual gain of material wealth. It is most difficult to "control the ego," which I interpret as critical self-reflection of our thought patterns and actions as they relate to the systems of domination within the coloniality of power. Therefore, "controlling one's ego" would mean developing a critical emotional intelligence that foregrounds long-term sustainable social and physical collective health. El vivir comunitario challenges the political economy of neoliberalism. On the notion of "espíritu," I return to the basic representation of "life." The word *spirit* comes from the Latin root *spirare*, which means 'to breathe.' Para hacer florecer el espíritu, one opens up to the connections we have to all forms of life that breathe, exchanging gases with one another as an inter-dependent manifestation that keeps us alive. By drawing upon our historical worldviews, students can draw from our community cultural wealth, as well as process the colonial practices we face. It behooves educational reformers to prioritize student voices as the primary approach to el vivir comunitario.

Working with younger generations has challenged me to look at myself and the interactions I have within my family. As a testament to living and learning in and outside formal spaces, our approach to developing emotional intelligence bleeds into every corner of educational settings. If I cannot embark on an active process within my family, I have no business as a facilitator of processing with "other" families with whom I work in the spirit of educational justice. After all, educational justice is intimately connected to organizing families as an integral approach that includes emotional intelligence as a connected unit toward communal wellness, el vivir comunitario, as a sustainable effort that can continue beyond the lifetimes of current activists. If we can build on recipes for tolerance, listening, dialogue, respect for oneself and others, and a critical understanding of socio-political forces that may influence our family social dynamics, we can fluidly shift our foci from micro-contexts to macro-socio-historical contexts. In the micro-context, we can focus on personal responsibilities and expectations of self-respect.

Oftentimes, as activists, we spend an incredible amount of energy (time, action, dialogue, organizing, etc.) in public spaces or organizations. We sometimes tend to lose ourselves in this activism, even while our families are in mayhem, finding themselves in a maelstrom of a space that is difficult to digest. We may think that by "saving the world," we are doing a charity act of some sort. In fact, our families may be the center of conflict, healthy conflict that must be addressed rather than avoided, ironed out rather than ignored, worked through rather than escaped, for it is in the nuclear status of our family dynamics that we find a force that can revolutionize the ways in which we approach educational change. We tend to isolate our educational experiences as students, parents, educators, administrators, researchers; we all have our own agendas and often we do not listen to one another to develop a common vision and plan to move forward.

When I went home that evening, I asked my pa about his experiences as a teenager and let him know about a sample of psychological issues that teens in US public schools may face today. When I asked him if he or anyone en el rancho allá donde vivía ever experienced anything similar, he resorted to meticulously describing el trabajo de la tierra, desde los tres años.... His story resonated with the stories of MEChA parents who had shared about their lifestyles as a youngster. After some reflection, I realized that my father was not confused about the role he played in his family or, by extension, his greater community en el rancho. His responsibilities matched the expectations of other young people as vital contributions to the survival of their families amidst a lack of opportunities to attend schooling institutions. While both contexts are different in time and space, the point to bring home here is that young people must have open avenues for developing their practices as strengths, processing their experiences as part of an integral development where students' voices are dignified and their practices contribute to the fabric of our community. Otherwise, students may feel trapped in their skin, silenced by confusion or denigrated as less than valuable.

Could it be that U.S.-urban-born generations are losing the relationship with the land that our parents lived cultivating? Could this relationship serve as one way to feed our understanding of the world, through physical activity and intergenerational connections? Would we develop a closer relationship to our foods if we grew them collectively? These were the fundamental questions that sprouted from the LDIR class that year. These questions laid the foundations for the revival of an abandoned lot on campus as a newfound space for food. We transformed a once run-down area into a vegetable and flower garden. I will tell you more about this inspiring yet challenging communal effort in Chapters 5 and 6.

Itzel participated in the CENS High School Scholar's Program during the summer, and she shared with students about JAVA, a programming language, and why participatory sensing might be useful for carrying on a campaign about something that was meaningful to them. We practiced using eight phones on loan from UCLA CENS to document our food and drink practices, rating them on how healthy we believed our food choices and availabilities were. I don't have the data for that summer anymore because we improvised while we were using a platform that was not designed for food choices. Nonetheless, Itzel led us to replace a Likert scale's terms to fit our own terms that were "in our heads," and to fill out the survey using our own understandings. The students agreed and began to document their eating habits. Later, Itzel and I would lead the reflection circles about our consumptions.

Later that year, as MEChA adult sponsors, we invited our colleague and ECS teacher, Mr. Adams, to join us for consideration for a UCLA Center X grant that would provide us with a space to bridge student activism with instruction in "formal" classroom spaces. The grant would provide us with an opportunity to collaborate over the content of our disciplines to "mobilize ancestral praxis, computer science learning, and student inquiry/engagement for communal wellness in El Sereno." After acceptance, this two-year grant, focused on teacher-initiated professional development, became a space for teachers to coordinate ways in which we could support student inquiry (see more on this collaboration in Chapter 5) across formal and informal spaces.

4.4   CONCLUSION AND FURTHER DISCUSSIONS

Sparked by the students, the process that we embarked upon was to re-seed MEChA on campus for the purposes of (1) promoting cultural awareness, (2) advancing college-going rates, and (3) connecting to the community. Cultural awareness, an informed sense of our shared history, became the primary force that connected us to others in and outside the school setting. Bringing forth our historical assets as an academic and artistic approach, our sense of our collective identities was the thrust that promoted activism on campus. Destendimos los rasgos de raíces ocultas en estas tierras, cementing a grounding of a positive sense of self. An estimated 600 people participated in our circle of activities during the school year, either during school assemblies, community workshops and events, Danza, and/or mesa meetings. As participants in the circle, we may never fully know how our collective efforts have affected one another. Learning happens in cycles. Scaffolding new information is processed over time, and each person digests new information differently. During my graduate years in Claremont, I took a class with Professor Lourdes Argüelles, entitled *Other ways of living, learning, and dying*. As the youngest in the group, I spoke minimally, but I was processing information and reflecting on my own experiences with the topics read and discussed by others. Years later, I find myself reverting to that space with a clear understanding about how the learning I absorbed from that class impacts the way I perceive the world today and my actions in it.

Because our MEChA community shared powerful spaces together, I am confident that each one of us who participated in our collective spaces took *something* with us on our respective journeys. In the next chapter, you will bear witness to the intricate webs of concentric circles of participation. While the complexity of our socially constructed worlds is too vast for the scope of this study, I will share links to the palpitation of influence we experienced altogether. However, I will also provide you with a laser-sharp focus on the learning ecology of the interactions between ancestral praxis and the computer science in the *Exploring Computer Science* classroom, Itzel's 6th-period class.

Because most the El Sereno schooling community originated in Mexico, and because the three adult MEChA sponsors also originated in Mexico, we focused on unearthing Mesoamerican ancestral praxis. This approach is limited because our schooling community includes families of Vietnamese, Hmong, European, African, and Pacific Islander descent. The participation of the Asian Pacific American Legal Center (APALC), a non-profit civil rights legal organization and sponsor of the Leadership Development in Interethnic Relations (LDIR) course, helps us make positive interethnic connections. I will address inter-ethnic ancestral praxis more in Chapter 6, when I describe the development of a community garden on campus, The People's Garden, an initiative by multiple groups that seeks to unearth ancestral connections to the land and our foods.

Let's call the process of re-discovering socio-histories (scientific, artistic, philosophical, etc.) in relation (or not) to colonial practices "ancestral praxis." You see, ancestral praxis sits in places; it is not unique to Mesoamerican peoples. We are all indigenous *somewhere*, and it is up to us to increase our awareness about our world so that we can transform the world through the word (Churchill, 1994; Freire, 1970). Learning about our ancestral worldviews does not promote "resentment to a group of people." It offers a window of self-awareness, while surveying how power has shifted over time and space, and thus allows us to question colonial systems.

The growing literature on inquiry-based teaching and learning sets the stage for students to be exposed to curricula and pedagogy that creates interest, generates curiosity, relates concepts to student knowledge and previous experiences, encourages students to investigate their own questions or interests, and asks students to justify their ideas in their own words through open-ended and probing questions. Oftentimes, educators are left without guidance on how to conduct inquiry-based teaching because teacher education programs are still heavily influenced by behaviorist teaching methodologies that do not draw on students' creativity for divergent thinking. Instead, the heavy emphasis of high-stakes testing pushes educators to "cover the standards" quickly with one-way directed learning.

It comes as no surprise to its advocates that inquiry-based teaching takes more time. This approach to teaching is tailored to each student's needs and more resources are needed. We cannot put the results in neatly designed charts and graphs, although there are more holistic ways in which we can measure student growth. This chapter has explored student-inquiry projects in an informal setting, a student-led organization on a comprehensive high school campus in El Sereno. Beginning with the microcosm of a student-led organization with a particular group of students who chose to make the time to develop leadership skills around something that was meaningful to them provides the stage for one of these students' development in the computer science classroom the following year. During her second year of leadership in MEChA, she learns computer science concepts and shares her leadership and learning with other students. Finally, MEChA's influence spawns into the classroom space and becomes the nexus for teacher collaboration. This spills over to the macro-context in a school and neighborhood-wide activity forum. The following two chapters describe how this happens.

Notes

1. What is known most commonly as Danza Azteca was introduced to the United States in the mid-1970s. It is an indigenous ritual cycle of dance that has roots deeply embedded in the ancient cultures of Mesoamerica (Aguilar, 2009). To identify as a Danzante is usually coupled with a level of commitment to keep the tradition alive.
2. A *cargo* is loosely translated as a contribution of individual efforts for the greater development of a community, an interdependent web of families.
3. A *copilli* is a feathered headdress that plumes a Danzante during Danza ceremony.
4. Nahuatl is an indigenous language of Anahuac, a derivative of the Yuto-Aztecan root of the Western Hemisphere.
5. Reserve Officers' Training Corps.
6. Mesa meetings were the organizing meetings of core MEChA members that took place off campus, usually on Tuesday nights.
7. Mesa meetings were the core organizing meetings attended by MEChA board members and sponsors.
8. We sang this song at our trip to Anahuac in the summer of 2011. For a small taste of our trip, see http://www.youtube.com/watch?v=pSpWZ7BRq1s&feature=colike.

References

Aguilar, M. (2009). *The rituals of kindness: The influence of the danza azteca tradition of Central Mexico on Chicano Mexcoehuani identity and sacred space* (Unpublished dissertation). Claremont Graduate University.

Anzaldúa, G. (1987). *Borderlands: The New Mestiza= La Frontera*. San Francisco: Spinsters/Aunt Lute.

Bowles, S., & Gintis, H. (1976). *Schooling in capitalist America: Educational reform and the contradictions of economic life*. New York: Basic Books.

Churchill, W. (1994). *Indians are us? Culture and genocide in native North America*. Monroe, ME: Common Courage Press.

Freire, P. (1970). *Pedagogy of the oppressed*. New York, NY: Herder and Herder.

Grosfoguel, R. (2010). Epistemic Islamophobia and colonial social sciences. *Human Architecture: Journal of the Sociology of Self-Knowledge*. Berkeley: University of California; Paris: Maison des Sciences de l'Homme (Ahead Publishing House).

Lareau, A. (2003). *Unequal childhoods: Class, race, and family life* (2nd ed.). Berkeley: University of California Press.

Marin, G. (2008, February 10). Los guerreros de la muerte florecida [Blog].

Marin, G. (2009, February 27). *Pedagogía Tolteca.* Paper presented at the California Association for Bilingual Education Annual Conference, Long Beach, CA.

Moreno Sandoval, C. D., Mojica Lagunas, R., Montelongo, L., & Díaz, M. (2016). Ancestral knowledge systems: A conceptual framework for decolonizing research in social science. *AlterNative: An International Journal of Indigenous Peoples, 12*(1), 18–31.

Olmeca. (2009). La contra cultura/counter culture: Pieces of me. Los Angeles: El Sereno, California.

Omi, M., & Winant, H. (1994). *Racial formation in the United States: From the 1960s to the 1990s (critical social thought)* (2nd ed.). New York: Routledge.

Paris, D. (2012). Culturally sustaining pedagogy: A needed change in stance, terminology, and practice. *Educational Researcher, 41*(93), 93–97.

Quijano, A. (2000). Coloniality of power and eurocentrism in Latin America. *International Sociology, 15*(2), 215–232.

Sfard, A., & Prusak, A. (2005). Telling identities: In search of an analyitic tool for investigating learning as a culturally shaped activity. *Educational Researcher, 34*(4), 14–22.

Somé, S. (1999). *The spirit of intimacy: Ancient teachings in the ways of relationships.* Green Forest, AR: Newleaf.

Somé, S. (2000). *The spirit of intimacy: Ancient African teachings in the ways of relationships* (1st ed.). New York: William Morrow Paperbacks.

Turkle, S. (2011). *Alone together: Why we expect more from technology and less from each other.* New York, NY: Basic Books.

Vaughan, D. (2002). Signals of interpretive work: The role of culture in a theory of practical action. In K. A. Cerulo (Ed.), *Culture in mind: Toward a sociology of culture and cognition* (pp. 28–54). New York: Routledge.

Vygotski, L. S. (1978). *Mind and society: The development of higher psychological processes.* Cambridge, MA: Harvard University Press.

Wenger, E. (2010). Communities of practice and social learning systems: The career of a concept. In C. Blackmore (Ed.), *Social learning systems and communities of practice* (Vol. x, Part III, pp. 179–198). London: Springer-Verlag.

CHAPTER 5

Cultivating Computing as Activism: Historicizing Cultural Identities as Academic Practices, 2010–2011

In this chapter, we **circle around the fire for a purpose**, and explore the **People's Garden**. As we brought our explorations and lessons outward into our ongoing lives, we found sustained cultivation, nourishment, and wisdom that continues to grow.

We explore **breaking the prison walls of restrictive schooling** through these new methods of exploration and inquiry, and through **student and teacher collaboration**. We also begin to dig into the data.

Explored by student activism during the 2009–2010 academic year, ancestral praxis bled into the *Exploring Computer Science* (ECS) classroom in 2010–2011 from four directions: Itzel, Mr. Adams, the ECS curriculum, and myself. This chapter describes the ways in which ancestral praxis spawned a learning ecology for cultivating positive cultural identities as academic practices within computer science learning. This section attempts to explore the sub-question: How do participants make sense of and act on ancestral praxis (AP) and computer science (CS) intersections[1] over time? We will see how Itzel drew from her prior historical knowledge systems and increased curiosities within the context of computing. We will bear witness to the growth in confidence, leadership, and cultural competence of the CS teacher, Mr. Allan Adams. And finally, we will follow the practice of computing as activism within a participatory sensing campaign spearheaded by Itzel and others on food and drink practices in our schooling community. The activities described in this chapter meet at the intersections of ancestral praxis and computer

© The Author(s) 2019
C. D. M. Sandoval, *Ancestral Knowledge Meets Computer
Science Education*, Postcolonial Studies in Education,
https://doi.org/10.1057/978-1-137-47520-6_5

science in that they exist within the context of nurturing positive cultural historical identities as academic practices, rather than the all-too-common approach of coloring a field devoid of a multiplicity of knowledge representations with tokenized versions of cultural representations. The activities promoted a critical self-reflexive practice for classroom participants who were willing to explore themselves. These developments led to promoting awareness to the larger schooling community (described in Chapter 6) of our newfound collective knowledge.

5.1   CULTIVATING CULTURAL IDENTITIES
AS ACADEMIC PRACTICES

During the summer of 2010, Itzel began her exploration of computer science learning through her participation in the UCLA CENS High School Scholars Program, where she joined a group of mostly underrepresented minority groups at the university lab. Her first impressions challenged her to visualize herself as a programmer. "I was looking at the JAVA codes and JAVA programming and all of the stuff like that and I was like 'what is this?! How am I going to make up a code?!'" She was relieved to see other students that she could relate to, "I felt nice too that there was the people from Puerto Rico. I was like, ok, I'm not the only Latina here." Yet she still felt "lost, like I don't know how I'm going to do this. I don't know how I'm going to make a different language with so many different letters and numbers and signs and stuff."

Her main task during the eight weeks of participation was to cooperatively design, program, and implement a participatory sensing campaign using mobile technology to collect data of wasted energy. She was grouped with two male students. And for the first time, she named the divisive structures of social inequity. For example, she was visibly upset when both her male team members would expect her to do the menial tasks of the project and, after she had worked long hours at the lab without their support, they took credit for her work: "I was like, 'how are you just like not doing anything, you left early the day before and you're just going to sit down and we still need to do the coding.' I was so mad!" I encouraged her to say something to her teammates or to someone she trusted in the program. Although she was challenged to voice her concerns about the unequal distributions of labor in her team, she also felt intimidated by the content. In the end, she was proud of her accomplishments and proudly presented her contributions to the participatory sensing campaign to bring about awareness of energy wasted while making a call to action to help energy-conservation efforts. This experience furthered her interest in digital technology to invigorate a social purpose that would provide meaning to her passions.

Her confidence in computer science learning increased as she gathered with the MEChA students in the evenings a few nights per week that summer. During this time, she shared some of the components she was learning at UCLA with an audience that had less exposure to computer science than she did, so she was automatically an expert in the group. We piloted a DietSens campaign using mobile eight phones that we borrowed from CENS. Itzel led the other MEChISTAS through the process of a participatory sensing campaign. We knew that DietSens would run in full effect during the academic year, so our chance to practice was during the summer. Itzel would often bust out her notebook and break it down for the group, teaching us a little bit of JavaScript and her data collection to share the process of research. During that time, Itzel asked her counselor to enroll her in *Exploring Computer Science* for the 2010–2011 academic year, a course offered in her small learning community, Mule Business & Technology Academy.

Itzel brought her summer participation in the UCLA CENS High School Scholar's program as a researcher in a nationally recognized university lab with other underrepresented minority scholars in computer science. She entered ECS with some background in hands-on computer science research, having piloting two participatory sensing campaigns: Save It! and DietSens. Although she did not feel confident in her skills as a coder, she was fluid with the potential societal implications of coding. The knowledge she carried spawned her approach to learning more about computer science and its power as a tool for social change. Both campaigns were designed with her participation in two circles, UCLA CENS scholars and Lomas High School MEChA scholars. Both CS projects were designed to promote awareness about the way we use (or waste) energy and our current food and drink practices. So, when she spoke to her counselor about enrolling in *Exploring Computer Science*, she had already completed a level of computing that few students with similar demographics had had the opportunity to access.

When Itzel "entered" ECS, she felt that "it was just worksheets…I was thinking this class was too easy, but it started going up." The first two units (of six) of the course consisted of exploring human–computer interactions and practicing problem-solving skills. Itzel and her peers practiced problem-solving dexterities together, usually through mathematical concepts. Most of the activities in the curriculum, as orchestrated by ECS teacher Mr. Adams, were geared toward group work in the spirit of a student inquiry-based approach to learning. Through algorithmic problem-solving skills, students were exposed to multiple ways of approaching a problem. After all, it is through the diagnosing of a problem that one can think about how (if at all) computer science can be used as a tool to solve a problem.

Students were exposed to problems that are not typical of most computer science classes. The first two units set the stage for students to think about computer science as a field where innovation and problem-solving are central to its focus. The Exploring Computer Science approach is not heavily focused on programming, as traditional computer science courses can be. Instead, students are exposed to opportunities where they can draw from issues that are meaningful to them and provide a space creative ways at solving problems. For example, in one lesson, students are asked to figure out the most "efficient" way of traveling from one city to various areas, considering multiple restrictions. However, because it was Mr. Adams' second year of teaching a not-so-familiar subject to him with a not-so-familiar pedagogical approach, he admitted to a sharp learning curve in both teaching and content. Besides, while it was his eighth year teaching, he had never received personalized coaching. ECS offered him a comprehensive program that supported his teaching through one-on-one coaching sessions by Suzanne, a computer science expert. In addition, the team of researchers in ECS prepared a series of professional development sessions at UCLA where teachers participated in hands-on activities that promoted inquiry-based instruction, equitable practices and computer science concepts.

There were a few instances when the ECS curriculum offered opportunities to make explicit connections between ancestral praxis and computer science concepts. The culturally situated design tools (Eglash, 2003) introduced at the beginning of the year in units one and two show a connection between ancestral praxis and computer science concepts. For example, the lessons of African and Native ancestry were designed to promote an exploration of computers as a tool for visualizing data, modeling and design, and art in the context of computer science. Furthermore, the tools offered students an opportunity to explore the cultural connections of weaving, beading, and braiding with digital simulations through mathematical concepts of these complex academic cultural systems. Mr. Adams considered me the cultural expert, since my unique positionality mirrored that of the students. He invited me to share cultural connections to the goal of the lesson. I prepared a session that invited students to reflect on previously taught computer science concepts from the first two units and the learning behind the culturally situated design tools. For example, after informally surveying the various cultural origins of students, I created a collage of ancient archaeological structures that were found in the spaces where students' families may have originated. We saw two short video clips that brought ancestral knowledge systems to the forefront of computer science inquiry. The first video was on Ron Eglash's TED talk describing African architecture as an example of geometric fractals. The second one showed a group of families that were concerned about the younger generations losing their ancient weaving practice to the commodities of "modernity."

I asked students to think about their families' histories when considering the questions: "How has my family background contributed to knowledge today? What tools have been used over time to solve societal problems?" When Itzel reflected on her families' ancestral praxis in the context of computer science, she shared her insight about the ways in which she saw the connections:

> I think it's the same as recycling. If there's something that we didn't know but that our ancestors knew, we've been recycling all these years until now because we still know about them. And there had to be some type of computer science. Probably not computers, but science and math back then for us to even put it together. There is some connection.

Itzel saw the evolution of knowledge as one that followed a line of thinking that built on science over time. She attributed the "science and math back then" as a foundation to the production of computer science today. And she mentioned, "us" as those that "put it together," referring to CS today. She included herself as part of the group that "put[s] it together," which embodies her identity as a contributor to knowledge. This is particularly significant for nondominant groups who lack representation in computer science, one of the most segregated fields in education. She saw her ancestors' knowledge systems evolve into computer science thinking. She also pushed the class to question whether we needed computers to follow the teachings of our family members. Regarding weaving she wrote, "We don't need a machine for that." When she shared these thoughts with her classmates, a discussion ensued about the gains and losses of using computers for certain tasks.

Computer science can be appropriated for meaningful operations within a community of practice that questions its use critically. For example, Crisis Informatics[2] is a new area of research that looks at the technical, social, and informational aspects of technology creation and implementation, particularly during crisis situations such as natural disasters. Itzel was sharply attuned to the social implications of computing, an approach that maintained her connections to her family and to history.

Just before Itzel graduated, I asked her to describe herself by using the phrase "I am" at the beginning of her self-ascribing expressions. She said, "I am a daughter, a creator, a sister, a producer, a learner, a consumer, a scientist, even though I'm not great at that, a mathematician...." She saw herself as a family member, first and foremost. She did not have to negotiate her identity as one that was connected to those that she cared most about. It is interesting that she did not mention computer science, although she did mention science and mathematics. Her leadership throughout the year demonstrated her increased confidence in relegating tasks to her teammates in a few occasions, male students of Chinese and Vietnamese-descent. Her leadership defied the common stereotypes of students of Chinese descent who may be considered the keepers of math and science knowledge at Lomas High School, following the model minority myth. With her confidence and diligence, Itzel led the class into thinking about our families' intellectual merit. She saw herself as a "scientist," even though she felt that she was "not great at that." She demonstrated her ease with calculation, however. For example, during the "Muddy City[3]" activity, Itzel was teamed with her usual group of two males. She called out her calculations to the whole class on several occasions to cross-check her answers with members of her group.

My field notes indicate that her ambition toward arriving at a solution became apparent. "Itzel dove into her sheet, making quick calculations by hand to arrive at the most cost-effective and shortest distance between the cities that must be visited on the trip. She asked Felipe across the room how he arrived at his answer and recalculated her response to show how Felipe misinterpreted the goal of the assignment. Felipe protested her result, as if he were upset that he did not get it right the first time. Albert, sitting next her, confirmed Itzel's findings and told Felipe that he was looking at the problem in a different way. In the end, Itzel accepted his approach by saying, "There's more than one way of getting an answer, we just have to think about how we got there and if it works." Itzel's authority on the mathematical calculations that involve computer science thinking illustrated her identity as a scientist and mathematician.

In his work with African-descent students and mathematics, Danny Martin (2000) affirmed that students with a positive sense of ethnic identity coupled an identity as a *doer* of mathematics results in positive learning experiences in segregated fields such as STEM[4] and computing. This research equipped youth to become daily activists in their subtle "performative" practices. Perhaps these practices included the development of the normative practices of science, such as developing standard scientific language that stems from Eurocentric "academic language," while retaining non-Eurocentric academic linguistic repertoires on equal footing. Itzel did not feel confident about her Eurocentric linguistic repertoires, which was the language spoken the in UCLA CENS laboratory with other computer scientists who did not necessarily look like her. She knew, however, that there was added value to her increasing knowledge of computer science concepts as a tool for social change in her community. Itzel's activism became more visible through her cultivation of DietSens, our participatory sensing research design and campaign for el vivir comunitario.

5.2   Confidence, Leadership, and Cultural Competence in Computer Science Teaching

At the time of our study, Mr. Adams was credentialed in Chemistry, Biology, Business Administration, and Multiple Subjects. He has a Master's degree in Business Administration, which may explain why business is his favorite class to teach. Prior to entering the teaching profession, Allan worked as a quality control overseer for 25 years, making sure that the food processing procedures were safe for eating. When he joined the Lomas High School teaching profession eight years ago as of 2010–2011, his teaching assignments included four content areas of preparation: Chemistry, Physical Science, Business, and Exploring Computer Science. As lead teacher of Mules Business and Technology Academy (MBTA), he advocated for the computer science class to be offered to the MBTA students because it is a college preparatory class that fulfills the "G"-credit requirement for the University of California.[5] As a result of his advocacy, he was allotted two sections to teach in 2010–2011. However, Mr. Adams was not credentialed to teach computer science. In fact, California does not have a pathway for teachers to receive an official credential in computer science. Research shows that it is common for CS teachers to be credentialed in other areas besides computer science (Goode, 2007). Yet, over time, despite the tall order placed upon him with various responsibilities, he has made some strides in developing his confidence in CS teaching.

Mr. Adams has attended nearly every professional development program that ECS offers at a university setting. Through a hands-on approach to developing content knowledge and pedagogy expertise, ECS created opportunities for CS teachers (who were most likely isolated as the single CS teacher on campus) to gather periodically and share their experiences. The coaching program provided Mr. Adams with a trusting relationship with Suzanne, a computer science expert who was trained in a Cognitive Coaching approach that works from the "inside-out" (Lindsey & MacDonnell, 2011), favoring a critical self-reflexive approach toward a teacher's self-discovery for sustainable growth. For the current academic year, Mr. Adams chose to focus on student engagement in his classroom. This meant that as a coach, Suzanne's role was to hold up a mirror for Mr. Adams to observe his practices that would support (or not) the engagement of his students.

At the beginning of the year, Mr. Adams was hesitant in providing students with explicit examples that taught computer science concepts as noted by "the example re 'conditionals in Scratch" Suzanne provided for him and "he did not run with it." In a March interview, Mr. Adams expressed trepidation about his teaching: "I don't know if it's really our, my role to try to make it all you know fun and games and all that kind of stuff." Yet by the end of the year, Mr. Adams demonstrated increased confidence in asking his students to look for connections between computer science and real-life applications. For example, Allan connected students' experiences in the school community garden to another community garden operated by the South-Central Farm in Los Angeles (not in the ECS curriculum). He asked students to reflect "on how you could have used something you learned in this class to help the farmers." This approach was a "breakthrough for him in both pedagogy and providing opportunities for students to engage in computational thinking," noted Suzanne in one of her reports. In addition to his opening to the issues that may be of high interest to his students, Allan reported that he was most excited about seeing kids get excited about using these tools and

> talk about how they like it or how they'll go to college and become an HTML expert based on what they learned here so that's pretty encouraging. I had a couple [students] last semester who were really into it, when we were doing the web browsing. Not very many, only a couple. I'm not an advanced programmer like some other teachers....

Rather than writing an evaluative end-of-year report on the themes I witnessed in this teaching in learning in ECS at Lomas, I decided to write him a letter that illustrated the cumulative nature of my observations over the course of my visits, which occurred on average twice a week over thirty-nine weeks, with each visit around 90 min. Following an action research model, I wanted to be as transparent with Mr. Adams as possible, again, to help hold a mirror up for him to notice his own teaching practices, as well as to listen to my perspective as a researcher activist. Here I have included an observation of his teaching computer science and one example of his interaction with Itzel.

> I noticed you guide students through trouble-shooting in HTML and Scratch to figure out why their code would not work properly or their sprite would not move in a certain direction. You explicitly told them to "try" different methods and asked them to think about their process as a meta-cognitive exercise. You pushed their thinking to demonstrate clear explanations to their thought-process. For example, when students were exposed to binary numbers, you asked them to write their thoughts in their journal to the question "How high can you count using your ten fingers?" And when Itzel responded "infinity" you asked her to explain her answer with the question "Can you really count up to infinity?" You validated their answers by writing them on the whiteboard and led the class in a discussion around problems, yet there was no clear conclusion in the end...There were some missed opportunities, especially to making connections to previous lessons. I suspect that becoming more familiar with the curriculum over the years will yield greater confidence to teaching the content while running common themes throughout so that students have a chance to make sense of computational thinking practices that build upon each other, rather than teaching them in isolation.

Since his first teacher training over a week-long ECS summer institute at UCLA in 2009, Mr. Adams mentioned that his small learning community was looking at ECS at his school as a model for technological advancements at his school. His enthusiasm for his participation in ECS seemed to provide him with an opportunity for teacher leadership at his school. Moreover, as the lead teacher of his small learning community, Mr. Adams accepted my invitation to participate in the Teacher-Initiated Inquiry Project (TIIP) sponsored by UCLA Center X. Although his role in the project the first year (2010–2011) was that of an active listener and conference participant at the Food Justice symposium in New Orleans, Louisiana, he was opening up to a whole new world by interacting with three self-identifying indigenous Xican@s: Mr. Floragon, Mr. Dueñas, and myself. We were very clear about the goals of the grant when we wrote it, collectively, as a team of four. In addition, Mr. Adams has emerged as a potential leader of technological advances at his small learning community since the positive review from the International Baccalaureate program, which may open opportunities for a greater focus on digital technology at his school, on a large scale. The possible expansion of ECS also must confront some challenges in terms of proper hardware resources.

Mr. Adams has also consistently reflected on the ways in which he has learned to "relate" to students, or "learn more about where they're coming from" as he develops cultural competence (Milner, 2011), alongside continued dialogue with the coach, other teachers, students, and the researcher: "At the beginning I would catch myself thinking that a student was a 'jerk' or 'immature.' One of the challenges that I face sometimes is not understanding how to work with kids in general. There's a lot of trial and error in that." Mr. Adams expressed his sincere reflections of his approach to working with "kids." He continued, "I forget how traumatic life can be as a teenager so I try to 'dig deeper' to find out what the real issue is if the student feels comfortable with me." When I asked him how he has seen his own growth over time, he said, "I am now more open about sharing my own personal challenges [with students], too." He recognizes that so much about his teaching is related to his personality. He likes to have students explore on their own without too much lecturing on his part as they both (teacher and student) gain confidence in the material. He "tries to be strategic" about the way he "presents an overview about the lesson and construct lessons" online so that the lessons can "stand on their own." In this way, he says, "the kids can get the basics so that they can explore and teach each other what they need to learn. It seems to work better that way than if I held their hand and showed them how to do every single thing." Mr. Adams expressed learning from Suzanne and me in the classroom: "I could see also from them is having a lot of personal contact with the kids and showing interest helps them [stay] motivated and on-task."

The curriculum is conducive for making space for students to explore particular content that they would be interested in sharing with a larger audience. For example, Mr. Adams reflects on his students' assignments and his developing cultural competence, "I remember one kid when we were doing Scratch who was from Vietnam, and he had a pretty intense story to tell about living in this community, so it was a pretty impressive story, and I could tell that he was pretty much into it." Another student, who was turned off the majority of the year, "lit up" with the Robotics units. About this student, Allan shared,

> ...there's one kid named Victor who didn't really have a lot of interest in the programming or a lot of the other things that we did. I could tell he was a smart guy. When it got to the robotics all of a sudden he became a superstar because he liked the mechanical part about it and he also did the programming and eventually he went up to an A from almost failing the first part of the semester. He definitely had the best robotic dance.

Allan admits that he has not "reached his happy moment" in his CS teaching. He is interested in developing content and increasing student engagement by "tapping into their backgrounds" and "making it fun for them." Here are some tenets that surfaced while taking note of his classroom practice and imagining a culturally sustaining pedagogy in computer science education (Table 5.1).

Oftentimes, the language around educational reform and teacher performance expresses an urgency that is reactionary, rather than foregrounding fertile ground for internal, sustainable growth, which may be slow in nature. There were also times when I caught myself slipping into a "missionary" approach to "helping" Mr. Adams with his teaching by "showing him" how it is done, as if my own style were a "one-size-fits-all" approach to perfect teaching. Although Mr. Adams did not engage much in ancestral praxis, he was actively listening in our TIIP meetings

Table 5.1 On culturally relevant Computer Science practices

Examples of colonizing schooling practices	*Examples of schooling practices para el vivir comunitario*
• Rote learning • Teacher-centered pedagogy • Divisive gender roles • Schooling for capital gain *only* • High-stakes testing culture • Competitive nature • Promoting individualism *only* • Motivation by grades *only* • Sink or swim mentality • Disconnected from socially responsible uses of technology • Glamorize digital tools as unquestioned solutions	• Creative, open-ended assignments • Inspire life-long learning • Balance independence and interdependence with others • Operate on ambiguous gender roles • De-center pedagogy • Promote curiosity • Expect excellence with clear expectations of all participants • Critical self-reflection • Scaffold learning

and during the conversations I would have with students about the potentiality of digesting the information and making sense of it for himself and his students as a way of validating historical academic practices that have existed for millennia.

Although Mr. Adams had not reached his happy moment in the classroom, his approach evolved over time. He began to see computing as a potential form of activism that could speak to the needs of the community in which he served.

5.3   Computing as Activism

By comparing food availability in El Sereno to Pasadena and South Pasadena, two neighboring areas with a higher average of income per household in 2009, the Leadership Development in Interethnic Relations students found that El Sereno fit the profile of a food desert, an area where healthy, affordable food is difficult to obtain. Instead of the abundant quality fresh foods that Pasadena and South Pasadena offered, El Sereno marked the presence of fast-food chains and liquor stores at various locations throughout the neighborhood. To continue with the spirit of Youth Participatory Action Research, the class combined this knowledge about food availability with other questions they sought to explore: "What do we eat?" and "Why do we eat what we eat?" Because MEChA and Chicanx Studies were interested in similar topics of inquiry, a collaboration ensued that would shape the next iteration of study. Itzel, Elisa, and Xochitl, three MEChA leaders and students in ECS and LDIR, participated in the research design. This is not a random sample. Participants were chosen if they were enrolled in the participating TIIP classes. However, unbeknownst to us, as the adult supporters and co-organizers of TIIP, the students' enrollment overlapped between MEChA membership and TIIP courses.

Do you see the connections? Students who were previously and concurrently involved in MEChA and LDIR activism had the opportunity to bring their passions to mark the center of study in ECS and LDIR projects. Adult support became crucial for Itzel to incorporate her family practices as a critical area of study in ECS. This approach to a culturally responsive and relevant pedagogy curriculum opened way for Itzel, Elisa, and Xochitl to collaborate with five adult educators to design the inquiry tool that would invite 75 other participants in LDIR and ECS to investigate their food/drink practices through DietSens. The DietSens research project was supported by the Center for Embedded Networked Sensing (CENS) at UCLA. Although students were not involved with the programming of the mobile application this time around, students were involved in the research design to gather the data and upload them onto a web server. After a series of after-school meetings with other students and educators, Itzel and Mr. Adams reported back to ECS just before the implementation phase of DietSens. Using mobile technology, the following ten open-ended and categorical items were co-constructed to explore the consuming of foods/drinks in our neighborhood:

1. Take a photo of food/drink you are about to consume.
2. What's on your mind about this food/drink?
3. In your opinion, how healthy is this food/drink?
4. Who do you eat this with?
5. Who chose this food/drink?
6. What food group does this primarily belong to?
7. Where was this food/drink prepared?
8. I eat/drink this food/drink (frequency)
9. This is how I feel when I eat/drink this
10. Why do I eat/drink this?

With the support of UCLA CENS, ECS introduced a participatory sensing campaign to collect data on the food/drink practices that students in three classes consumed. A total of 1557 entries were collected over one month during the spring of 2011. During the second week of data collection, we surveyed the words that the participants were using to describe what was on their mind about this food/drink. Itzel thought that this technique would appeal to a familiar platform to input data that was similar to updating a status on a social networking site by answering the question "What's on your mind about this food/drink?" with an open space for comments. After the first two weeks, we created a word cloud by using an application called Wordle[6] to visually represent the distribution of responses by giving prominence to the words that appeared with the highest frequency (Fig. 5.1).

It is interesting to note that the most popular words to describe what was on the mind of the consumer and documenter of the data were "I'm hungry" by the second week. The Center for Health Promotion and Wellness at MIT Medical School provides a Hunger Scale to describe common eating practices. On a Likert scale with numerical values that range from 1 to 10, the scale measures the levels of hunger one experiences. In her four-week session series of Healthy Eating workshops at UCLA, registered dietician Eve Lahijani introduced the hunger scale

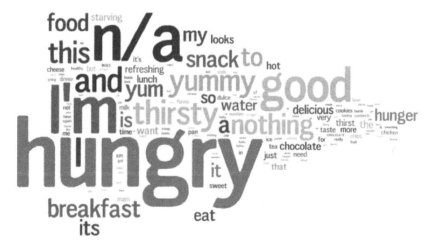

Fig. 5.1   Week 2 responses to "what's on your mind about this food/drink?"

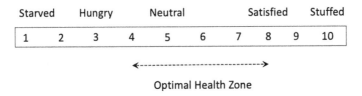

Fig. 5.2 Hunger scale (Adapted from the Center for Health Promotion and Wellness, MIT)

and provided evidence that one should eat at the very first signs of hunger, before entering the (1–3 zone) of hunger or feelings of starvation. Moreover, we should eat until we are comfortably satisfied (7–8), but not stuff ourselves into a food coma that may interfere with our energy levels (Fig. 5.2).

A study on centenarians (Wilcox, Wilcox, & Poon, 2011) found that food is best consumed at regular intervals throughout the day, avoiding strong feelings of hunger or starvation patterns. Eating until we feel no more than 80% full is ideal for optimal health. If participants are reporting feeling hungry, what implications may feelings of hunger have on learning? Physical activity? Emotional development? Building community? El hambre es cabrona, pero más el que la aguanta. What may seem like a small indicator of food practices in El Sereno can have larger implications for our general well-being as individuals who make up a schooling community. Why would anyone aguantarse and not eat? To be familiar with feelings of hunger may be a cue that perhaps there is a larger issue of food availability. Could it be that we can find ways to collectively pay attention to the foods/drinks we consume for optimal health as a community? Although we did not explore this topic in the depth that is possible, we did, nonetheless, look at basic descriptive statistics and surveyed the photos we were taking over the month of data collection. We discussed ailments such as hypertension, heart disease, and diabetes in our familias. We made some connections with what we were eating and its possible impact on our general well-being. Students used programming to tell a story that delivered a call-to-action for the viewers of their animation project using Scratch.

Two weeks later, during the last half of the study, the qualitative measure of the survey indicated that students reported "I'm hungry" most frequently about what was on their mind before consuming their food choices.

When young people experience hunger or multiple episodes of hunger, this can be associated with poorer general health conditions than their counterparts who are not experiencing hunger. Kirkpatrick, McIntyre, and Potestio (2010) examined the effects of hunger as an extreme manifestation of food insecurity on subsequent health outcomes using data spanning a ten-year period in the Canadian National Longitudinal Survey of Children and Youth (NLSCY). Children who reported ever being hungry and multiple episodes of hunger were associated with poorer general health compared to those who were never hungry. Higher odds of chronic asthmatic conditions were observed among youth who experienced multiple episodes of hunger. In the United States, 15% of households experienced food insecurity[7] in 2008, up from 11% in 2007, marking the highest prevalence recorded since national monitoring of food insecurity began in 1995 (Coleman-Jensen, Nord, Adams, & Carlson, 2008). While the computer science class did not learn about food politics in detail, when it was time for them to create computer science artifacts, some groups decided to address food politics within the DietSens project.

Using computer programming, four out of ten student groups chose to write their final Scratch projects related to the DietSens campaign. The other projects' areas exposed issues with tagging, graffiti, the use of lockers in school, littering, and a community park. Each project produced in the class left the audience with a call to action. All projects included a call to action for a specific audience. Some of the samples asked residents to help clean up the tagging and graffiti in the neighborhood, pick up trash, become more aware of the budget cuts and their effect on closing down El Sereno community park recreation program for teens after school, and the comparison between the state's investments into community parks and recreation over the prison industrial complex.

Scratch allows students to intuitively use color and categories to learn the basics of a graphical programming language. Developed by MIT, the name of the program alludes to the sounds one hears when spinning vinyl records on a turntable. Having the ability to mix different types of media clips, such as graphics, photos and audio, the program nurtures intellectual creativity among adolescents. For example, using mathematical and computational ideas such as coordinates, variables, and random numbers, students imagine an idea, create a working model, experiment with the model by debugging glitches, share the model, receive feedback, revise the model, and perhaps reimagine it for another cycle of computer science learning as algorithmic problem-solvers.

Itzel and her partner, Audrey, paired up to use programming as a means to share pertinent information about healthy food practices with the larger schooling community of El Sereno. They prepared a Scratch final project that would increase awareness about the foods that students were eating. Using complicated systems, Itzel and Audrey told a story about healthy food choices in our community that was accessible to their audience. The script begins with two cats at a grocery store, chatting about their food inquiries. The first cat wonders about what to buy for "this week's meals" and wonders where the Oreos and chips are located. Another cat shows up with a grocery cart filled with fresh fruits and vegetables, and asks about the location of the "red apples" that are "obviously not here" in the section in which the two cats meet. The next scene invokes reflection by sharing that "Kat reflects on his food choices," with a black background, and "He remembers that his parents have Diabetes and he should be eating healthier."

Then Kat transitions to sitting in the formal space of a classroom at school. Itzel and Audrey specifically situate the sprite's[8] learning about food practices to the formal institution of public schooling. They introduce another character, "Jeff," who comes from UCLA to teach them about participatory sensing. This uses mobile technology for data design and collection for the specific purpose of documenting food and drink practices that will help determine "what we eat, where it's from, and if it's healthy or not." The students ask Jeff about the phones they are to use for the project, "What if our phones don't have a camera?" Itzel and Audrey considered the socio-economic factors of their neighborhood and the limitations; a lack of resources could skew the outcome of the proposed project. One of the limitations of this section is that the students in ECS were not included as a participatory element of the design of the research study. As mentioned in Itzel and Audrey's script, Jeff came from UCLA to present the project to them, rather than having the students codesign the project. Due to time constraints, only Itzel represented the design of the research study. Ideally, we would have included much more time for the co-construction of the design as a triple-class force.

When Jeff announces that the students will be loaned smartphones by CENS, all students volunteer to participate. The script shows how excited students are about using technology. Kat goes off to document his foods and drinks over a month's time. As pair-programmers, Itzel and Audrey tell the story that emerged from the project (Fig. 5.3).

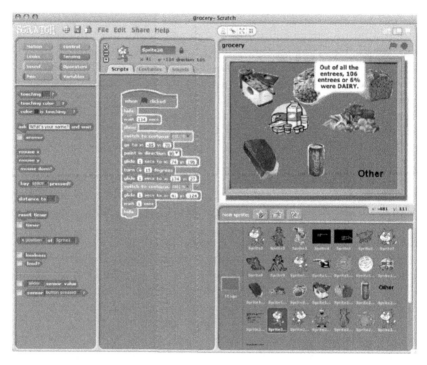

Fig. 5.3 Scratch final project, Itzel and Audrey, descriptive statistics for DietSens, 2011

They reported the frequencies of the food and drinks that were consumed according to food group (see Fig. 5.4) and preparation. As a result of the research study and conclusions, Kat is inspired to eat healthy foods. He switches from eating at McDonald's to purchasing food from organic markets. Although Itzel and Audrey decided to transmit the economic situation when the research study began by asking Jeff what they were to do if their phones did not have the capacity to take pictures, they did not make mention of the socio-economic difference between purchasing different types of foods in Fig. 5.5. Unbeknownst to the ECS class, which minimally investigated food deserts in class, the LDIR class might have told a story about access to healthy foods in their neighborhoods and problematized this statement. Is healthy, organic produce readily available to the El Sereno schooling community?

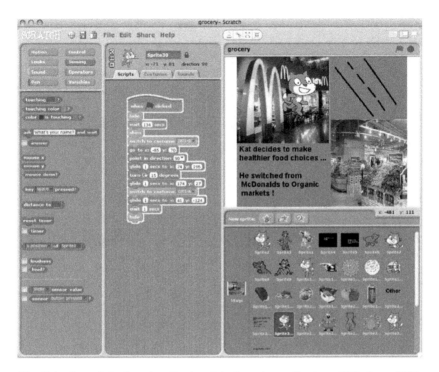

Fig. 5.4 Scratch final project, Itzel and Audrey, data collection of DietSens, 2011

The next scene shows Kat at home, addressing his parents and brother about what he learned in school about eating healthy foods. The following transcription takes place at Kat's home with his parents and brother:

[White letters on black solid background]
From this experience, we learn that what we eat today will affect our health.

Since Itzel had the most experience with investigating healthy foods in the community as a young scholar with MEChA and UCLA CENS, and now in ECS, she was able to apply her learning to a family setting that brought to life the realities of food and drink practices at home. She made clear connections to ancestral identity with food practices, using computer science as a tool to promote awareness about our historical food practices and its health correlates.

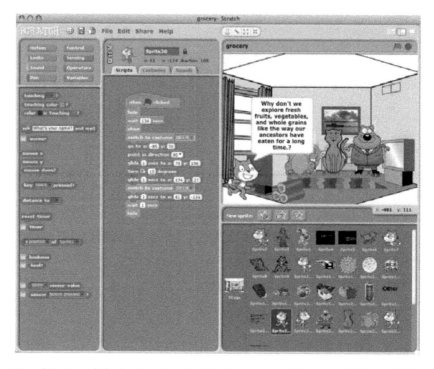

Fig. 5.5 Scratch final project, Itzel and Audrey, ancestral foodways, DietSens, 2011

[Scene transitions to Kat's house]

Kat: Hey Mom and Dad! I was involved with a food project at school and I have become worried of the ways we eat. I dont [*sic*] feel were eating healthy.

I think we should set an example for other families and begin eating healthier.

Perhaps thats [*sic*] why you're grumpy Dad... at work you only eat from fast food restaurants.

Mom: I don't doubt it.

Dad: You think so? I have been eating out a lot Dear is that so?

This section is perhaps the pinnacle of exploration to the foundational question of this study. Itzel connected ancestral praxis and computer science para el vivir comunitario. By making a connection from what she learned in MEChA in her computer science class, she increased her awareness about the critical history of food consumption in her family/ community. Then she took this understanding to her family, keeping the ancestral fire alive, cutting through present-day colonialism of the flesh (Anzaldúa, 1987).

> *Kat*: Why don't we explore fresh fruits, vegetables, and whole grains like the way our ancestors have eaten for a long time?
> *Mom*: You're right mijo.
> I can make excellent calabazitas!
> *Brother*: Mmmm Carnitas! Posole! Mole! Let's eat!
> *Kat*: No! I'm talking about 500 years ago before our diets were drastically changed!
> Come on, Bro! Those foods you mentioned are really foreign to us and they are making us sick...
> *Dad*: But they're so tasty and we all love them!
> Fine then.
> "Happy healthy eating!"
> *[The script ends with five smiling entities sharing a turkey dinner (four two-legged humans+ one four-legged Kat)]*

Itzel associated colonial foods (500 years to now) with foods that are "foreign to us and they are making us sick." When I read this, it took me back to conversations we had during our MEChA meetings at Xocolatl and in Kevin's classroom after school hours. Huitzilmazatzin, one of our community elders and caretakers of Classical Nahuatl, shared the history our ancestral foodways as we conceptualized our community garden on campus. While Itzel did not speak for the majority of the sessions, she voluntarily attended each one of the four conversations we had in the larger circle about ancestral foodways. Returning to Itzel's ancestral computing artifact, Itzel suggested that her family be an example for other families as they think about their food consumption critically by investigating the history of foods and "500 years ago before our diets drastically changed!" as a means to relate the community's food practices to the coloniality of power that pushed for the erasure of a slew of native foods and the introduction of foreign foods.

Exploring Computer Science and our shared participation provided a space for Itzel to foster ancestral computing practices that drew from her socio-historical experiences. Itzel's partner was able to learn from Itzel as her partner shared her concerns about diabetes in her family. Both partners created an animated representation of their research and data analysis. Their animation related to their personal experiences as a meaningful cognitive task that spoke about their families and schooling community. Research and data analysis requires technical and philosophical knowledge about statistics to tell a compelling story. Equipping students with these scientific norms helps prepare them for the twenty-first century as they develop as citizen scientists. DietSens became a venue for us to wonder about our eating patterns while investigating the socio-political story of food in our community. I decided to explore the data using three variables that were associated to the social, physical and feelings about our food practices. Table 5.2 shows descriptive statistics of the three variables that I explored for this dataset.

Of the 1557 data entries by 51 teens and 4 adults, 62% reported eating alone while 24% reported eating with their families. Forty percent of the food consumed was prepared at home while 35% was commercially packaged. Fifty-five percent of the participants reported positive feelings

Table 5.2 Frequencies and percentages of DietSens Data Q4, 7 & 9, March 29–April 29, 2011

	Family	Friend	Alone	Other	N/A
Q4 Who do you eat this with?	372	183	972	26	4
	24%	12%	62%	2%	0%

	Home	Restaurant	Commercially Packaged	Fast Food	School	Street	Other	N/A
Q7 Where was food prepared?	629	101	546	119	70	24	59	9
	40%	6%	35%	8%	4%	2%	4%	1%

	Positive	Neutral	Negative	Other
Q9 This is how I feel when I eat/drink this	855	581	110	12
	55%	37%	7%	1%

	Teens	Adults	Total		LDIR	ECS
Respondents	51	4	55		37	18
Entries	1377	180	1557		1282	275

Table 5.3 Percentage distribution of food preparation and together/alone on feelings

| Feel when eat | Eating together/alone and Cooked/packaged foods | | | | Total |
| | ------Eating alone------ | | ------Eating together------ | | |
	Packaged	Cooked	Packaged	Cooked	
Negative	50	3	38	14	105
	10.53%	0.70%	16.24%	4.86%	
Neutral	201	134	103	101	539
	42.32%	31.16%	44.02%	35.07%	
Positive	224	293	93	173	783
	47.16%	68.14%	39.74%	60.07%	
Total	475	430	234	288	1427

when eating or drinking while 7% reported negative feelings. After looking at the descriptive statistics, I wanted to see if there was an association between the variables.

Table 5.3 is a three-way contingency table of the variables that indicate feelings when eating, where the food was prepared and food consumption with others/alone. For purposes of this analysis, I did not differentiate between food and drink. As you can see, the most compelling associations exist between participants who reported feeling positive when eating cooked food alone (68.14%) as opposed to reporting positive feelings when eating packaged food with others (39.74%). Overall, respondents who ate cooked food that included home-prepared meals or food made in restaurants were more likely to report positive feelings about it than respondents who ate packaged food (commercially packaged food, fast food, or school food). Surprisingly, respondents who were eating alone were more likely to report positive feelings than respondents who were eating with others. Remember that 51 of the 55 participants were adolescents. This could mean that teenagers prefer to be by themselves rather than with friends or family. I believe this is an area we could open up for dialogue in the classes that conducted this research to explore our campaigning efforts toward el vivir comunitario.

Another interesting finding draws upon the small sample of reported negative feelings when consuming food. Respondents were more likely to report negative feelings about eating when they consumed packaged foods as opposed to cooked foods, whether these were eaten alone (10.53%) or with others (16.24%).

To test the further significance of relationships reported in Table 5.3, I conducted a multinomial logistic regression. Table 5.4 illustrates the results of the multinomial logistic regression that allows us to see whether there is a statistically significant interaction between the two independent variables—food preparation and consumption with others—on the outcome variable, feelings about food consumption. This type of regression estimates the effect of independent variables on the log-odds of having a certain outcome relative to an omitted category of the outcome. It is similar to a binomial logistic regression, but the dependent variable has more than two categories. Upon calculations, the results are statistically significant at $p < 0.05$ level, meaning that we can make a claim that, in the general population, these results are not due to chance. For example, the estimated log-odds of eating commercially packaged food together decreases the likelihood of feeling positive rather than negative by 0.8 points. But eating cooked food alone increases the estimated log odds of feeling positive rather than negative by two points.

Respondents favored home-prepared food and eating in restaurants more than eating commercially packaged, school, street, or fast food. But why do teens prefer eating alone? What if there's a difference between reporting eating with family than eating with friends? And, because I collapsed these two categories under "eating together," I may have skewed results. To address these two issues, I did further analysis and, in fact, I found there was no significant difference between reporting eating with

Table 5.4 Multinomial logistic regression predicting feelings on eating together vs. alone and eating cooked vs. commercially packaged foods, March 29–April 29, 2011

Feel when eat	Coefficient	Std. error	z	P>|z|	[95% Conf. interval]	
Negative			base (out come)			
Neutral						
together	−0.5987	0.2180	−2.75	0.006	−1.0259	0.1715
cooked	1.4489	0.2805	5.17	0.000	0.8992	1.9986
_cons	1.4823	0.1562	9.49	0.000	1.1762	1.7884
Positive						
together	−0.8366	0.2169	−3.86	0.000	−1.2616	−0.4116
cooked	2.1146	0.2771	7.63	0.000	1.5716	2.6577
_cons	1.5977	0.1545	10.34	0.000	1.2948	1.9007

family or friends. Eating with friends and eating with family pointed to similar results: an increase in estimated log odds of feeling negative rather than positive, independent of each other. Adolescents simply prefer to eat alone. Over 62% of respondents reported eating alone, and 50% of the DietSens respondents felt positive when eating. Based on these and additional findings, we can find an informed approach to continuing our participatory action research that cultivates the visions of our community. For example, we might use these data to promote home-cooked meals on campus.

These empirical findings could lead to greater questions about the food and drink practices that were captured by the data collected. Further analysis is needed in this area, to take into account interactions between other variables that were tested last year, as well as the results' connections to the individual participants themselves. The next phase of the data analysis and campaign design will be collectively collaborated with other scholars in ECS, LDIR, and Chicanx Studies: teachers, students, and community members alike. Making sense of the data should be a communal effort by the participants who make up a part of this study. In the spirit of Youth Participatory Action Research, we will conduct more research in this area, collectively, so as to best strategize a campaign that takes into account the data and a call to action para el vivir comunitario.

Critical computer science involves a socio-historical approach to learning. While students were not involved in the latter part of the DietSens analysis, I have presented one possible outcome of data analysis. Analyzing and visualizing data is a core tenant of computer science learning. Ultimately, the data can be utilized to spawn a call for action that is supported by empirical research. However, at this point, I hesitate to go further into the analysis until I can collaborate on the data with other scholars in ECS, LDIR, and Chicanx Studies, teachers, students, and community members for a community of scholars can best determine the next courses in a campaign, than only one person alone. Similarly, digital tools can be seen as the panacea to common societal problems. Technophilia points to practices that rush to digital production as a "savior" to societal problems.

5.4   DISCUSSION

I do not intend to separate ancestral praxis practices from computer science learning. In fact, I consider them similar in that both are based on logical thinking and observational phenomena. Yet we tend to look at both disciplines as opposites. We may perceive ancestral praxis as "ancient" and computer science as "modern," yet both maintain existing networks for a specific purpose. Ancestral praxis maintains the encapsulation of a complex world that directly responds to the immediate needs of the people in conjunction with the environment. Over time, as globalization has increased, these disciplines overlap in concentric circles of practice, Figured Worlds (Holland & Lachiotte, 1998). These are not separate, in that they both deserving of equal intellectual merit, as is all knowledge-re-producing practices. We should not place more value on one over the other, such as projecting that if we knew computer science well (creating HTML, coding, data analysis, etc.), we would have a more competitive computational force. Yet if we do not consider, for example, the socio-historical, environmentally sustainable advances that computer science does not emphasize enough, then we will continue a systemic denial of a multiplicity of knowledges, which is the foundation of our society. So, for starters, let's consider ancestral praxis and computer science on equal footing, both as contested spaces and tools for recreating knowledge today.

The situated action of the participants of this study "offer no prescription because there is no prescription" (Martin & McGee, 2009, p. 212) to other communities of practice. The specific context in which I offer the narrative of Itzel's learning processes within the context of the computer science classroom demonstrates that computer science learning does not happen in isolation. Life experiences as a Mexican American female, often characterized by marginalization and resistance makes it difficult to maintain a positive sense of self in the pursuit of computer science knowledge. Yet typifying these same struggles, as Martin (2007) noted for African American students learning mathematics, "can be transformative in terms of one's identity when those struggles are put in the context of liberation and freedom, and these become the motivators" (p. 157) to pursue computer science knowledge and meaningful participation. Itzel did not have to compromise her identity when she learned about the mathematics behind braid making in class. Her presentation on cornrow braids demonstrated that she took leadership in learning the richness behind the geometric and iterative processes that involved braid making. For her final presentation, Itzel simulated a hairstyle using a programming software developed at the Rensselaer Polytechnic Institute. She said, "I never thought cornrows had anything to do with coordinates...." When she presented her final project to the class, she told a story that incorporated the history of cornrows in the African-descent community. In hindsight, when she reflected on her learning, she said that prior to the cornrow activity in the computer science class, she "didn't know why the [braids] were so important. I just thought they were a braid in their hair. I didn't really think it was important, or that there was a story [behind the braiding]. I just thought it was a hairstyle." When she learned about the connections to mathematics and computer science concepts, she said, "Then you go into x, y, and their braiding while they are telling the story. Or there's a meaning for every braid, and there's special ceremonies and special events [for] different braids. That's meaningful."

She was given a venue to learn mathematical and computer science concepts within a context that was familiar to her. Although cornrows are not part of her family practice, braiding hair has been part of her family practice "for generations." Using online software to create braids on coordinates, the activity enabled Itzel and her classmates to apply the problem-solving process that inextricably shapes computing fields. Itzel created patterns that used standard design tools to visually represent simulations of braids on human hair. In addition, Itzel determined if a given solution successfully solved the stated problem.

Itzel and others dignified their participation in computing without compromising ancestral ways of knowing. While making sense of her identity through her participation in MEChA as a simultaneous activity to Exploring Computer Science, Itzel was able to bring her identity as a storyteller while exploring computing. Itzel, as part of a particular community (that has traditionally been excluded from computing) has come to "own" computing and apply it to something that is of great importance to her community. Computing is no longer an "outside" entity; it is something that has been shaped into a space for social activism that is relevant to her, not something "imposed" but something "recreated" to foster community healing.

Furthermore, Itzel's leadership planted seeds of critical ancestral computing for the protection of mother earth (Moreno Sandoval, 2017) and community healing as you will read in the next chapter.

NOTES

1. As described in Chapter 2, ancestral praxis and computer science intersections are is also called ancestral computing. I use both forms interchangeably.
2. More information can be found at http://www.cs.colorado.edu/~palen/Home/Crisis_Informatics.html.
3. Muddy City is an example from Computer Science Unplugged and is used to introduce algorithms, minimal spanning trees, Dijkstra's algorithm, and collaborative problem solving. For more information see http://csunplugged.org/minimal-spanning-trees.
4. STEM is an acronym for fields of study in science, technology, engineering, and mathematics.
5. "G" credit fulfills the University of California requirements for a college preparatory elective course. For more information see http://www.ucop.edu/a-gGuide/ag/a-g/elective.html.
6. http://wordle.net/.
7. Food insecurity exists when there is a lack of nutritionally adequate and safe foods.
8. Kat is a sprite in Scratch. In this case, the sprite is a cat that acts as the protagonist of the animated project.

REFERENCES

Anzaldúa, G. E. (1987). *Borderlands: The New Mestiza = La Frontera.* San Francisco: Spinsters/Aunt Lute.

Coleman-Jensen, A., Nord, M., Adams, M., & Carlson, S. (2008). *Household food security in the United States.* Washington, DC: Economic Research Service, United States Department of Agriculture.

Eglash, R. (Producer). (2003). *Culturally situated design tools: Teaching math and computing through culture.* Troy, NY: Rensselaer Polytechnic Institute.

Goode, J. (2007). If you build teachers, will students come? The role of teachers in broadening computer science learning for urban youth. *Journal of Educational Computing Research, 36*(1), 65–88.

Holland, D., & Lachiotte, W., Jr. (1998). *Identity and agency in cultural worlds.* Cambridge, MA: Harvard University Press.

Kirkpatrick, S., McIntyre, L., & Potestio, M. (2010). Child hunger and long-term adverse consequences for health. *Archives of Pediatrics & Adolescent Medicine, 164*(8), 754–762.

Lindsey, D. B., & MacDonnell, L. (2011). The inside-out approach. *Journal of Staff Development, 32*(1), 34–38.

Martin, D. B. (2000). *Mathematics success and failure among African-American youth: The roles of sociohistorical context, community forces, school influence, and individual agency.* Mahwah, NJ: Lawrence Erlbaum.

Martin, D. B. (2007). Mathematics learning and participation in the African American context: The co-construction of identity in two intersecting realms of experience. In N. S. Nasir & P. Cobb (Eds.), *Improving access to mathematics.* New York and London: Teachers College Columbia University.

Martin, D. B., & McGee, E. O. (2009). Mathematics literacy for liberation: Reframing mathematics education for African American children. In B. Greer, S. Mukhophadhay, S. Nelson-Barber, & A. Powell (Eds.), *Culturally responsive mathematics education* (pp. 207–238). New York: Routledge.

Milner, H. R. (2011). Culturally relevant pedagogy in a diverse urban classroom. *Urban Review, 43,* 66–89.

Moreno Sandoval, C. D. (2017). Critical ancestral computing for the protection of Mother Earth. In C. Coulter & M. Jiménez-Silva (Eds.), *Culturally sustaining and revitalizing pedagogies: Language, culture and power* (pp. 25–40). Bingley, UK: Emerald Publishing Limited.

Wilcox, D. C., Wilcox, B. J., & Poon, L. W. (2011). Centenarian studies: Important contributors to our understanding of the aging process and longevity. *Current Gerontology and Geriatrics Research, 2010,* 1–6.

CHAPTER 6

Spreading Seeds of Hope from Student-Led Initiatives to Classroom Practices para el Vivir Comunitario, 2011–2012

In this chapter, we focus on **Our Earth, Our Bodies: Building Our Future with Dignity**. We do this, in part, by working toward **ancestral computing for sustainability,** meaning that programs growing out of these studies can be implemented in other neighborhoods, with different (and similar) pressures and struggles, and result in healthier, more connected communities.

We also explore implications for other school sites, shortcomings of this early model, and further imagine utilizing ancestral praxis to undo community damage and re-gift our identities to ourselves.

Since the first day of our collective MEChA meeting at Xocolatl in January 2009, Dora's interest in feeding the homeless on Skid Row would feed movement of food justice in the schooling neighborhood of East Los Angeles. Although the movimiento did not start with MEChA, nor is it dependent on MEChA, it was fed by a positive sense of self, creatively and academically. The LDIR–Chicanx Studies–ECS trio of classes continues its dedication toward building a sustainable ecology of learning about ancestral praxis, computer science, and critical consciousness of food justice and health. In this way, learning exists within the context of our family histories and a critical consciousness about the confluences that have led us to the particular context we live in now (e.g., understanding the food desert in which we live, learning programming as an underrepresented minority in this field, re-awakening our relationship with the land by growing ancestral foods as a decolonizing practice). Student inquiry

© The Author(s) 2019
C. D. M. Sandoval, *Ancestral Knowledge Meets Computer Science Education*, Postcolonial Studies in Education,
https://doi.org/10.1057/978-1-137-47520-6_6

is vital to the centripetal force of this movement, cultivated by adult support and institutional backing. Together, students, teachers, parents, and community members co-constructed a new way of thinking about computer science education: critical ancestral computing for the protection of Mother Earth, toward a responsible way of producing technology from the worldviews of Indigenous peoples (Moreno Sandoval, 2017; Moreno Sandoval, Mojica Lagunas, Montelongo, & Díaz 2016).

6.1   Dignified Teaching as Collaborative Actors for Educational Excellence

Adult support of student inquiry spawns the ways in which young people remain engaged in educational excellence. Yet the intersectional rights of adults must be supported by institutional avenues as well (Moreno Sandoval, Hernández-Saca, & Tefera, 2017). This does not happen easily because of the pressure that institutions and adults receive from the state that is focused on high-stakes testing as one of the only measures of student success. Even though none of the three classes involved in this study (LDIR, Chicanx Studies, and ECS) are required to take a state test in that area of study, the climate of urban schooling is dictated by these measures. For example, the school was threatened to be taken over by the state in 2017 because, like most other high schools in Los Angeles, it had not met the NCLB-mandated proficiency goals in testing. So, the schools across three neighboring El Sereno campuses decided to apply for an International Baccalaureate status. The year 2018, the final year of review for this application process, remains hopeful for the three schools to be recognized as IB schools. This may allow them to be considered in different standing with the state, as autonomous schools with academic content that expands the narrow focus of California standards. Since IB status would require an increased focus on computer science, Mr. Adams was inspired to sign up for an E-learning Instructional Design course online with the University of California Irvine. His teaching approach has become more flexible with his increased confidence in teaching Computer Science. This year, at the students' request, he has opened up an opportunity for students to choose which program they are willing to learn more about (Scratch, Flash, or HTML) in their final projects, whereas the structure of the class did not allow students to make those types of decisions before.

In addition to his increased flexibility, Mr. Adams has accepted our request that he take on the lead teacher role in our TIIP grant. This requires that he make sure our paperwork is in place, our online portfolio is complete, and our communication with UCLA staff remains clear. This has given him an added sense of confidence in his contributions to the team. A strong community is comprised of strong individuals who give for the greater benefit of the whole. This is counterintuitive to the capitalist meritocracy to which we are conditioned in schools as we continue on our individual journeys in this country.

One of our collective projects brought students, teachers, administrative staff, parents, and community members together. They came to see *The Children of the Plumed Serpent* exhibit on Ancient Mexico at the Los Angeles County Museum of Art. As he prepared for the trip, Mr. Adams created a space for students to compare computational artifacts from present-day tools.

In addition to larger-community activities, Kevin, lead teacher at Lomas High School, spear-headed a conscious hip-hop club after school to meet with the Tree Club, which cares for The People's Garden on campus. Rudy maintains MEChA's activism on campus. These clubs come together as "Urban Visionaries" to feed creative practices and expressions within the high school community. Their common meeting place is the community garden that was created on campus as a result of these collaborations.

6.2   Keeping the Fire Alive Within Imagined Community

Itzel enrolled at the University of California Santa Cruz in fall 2011. She declared her major as sociology, a bit different than her senior plan of communications. In the first quarter, she enrolled in *Intro to Sociology*, a writing class "to help my papers," and some core classes that are required by the university. It took a bit of adjustment to the drastic change of living on the other side of California. She was missing home quite often and found herself getting sick; she had to rely on her friends and herself to get better. She did not join any organization, as the level of study her classes required was different than what she was used to at Lomas High School. Nonetheless, she completed her first quarter and soon came home during winter break to spend time with her familia and friends. Despite feeling homesick with the sharp transition into a new environment that was culturally different than her familiar comfort level, Itzel returned the second quarter with an enthusiasm that she brought from home. She enrolled in a nutritional biology class as well as *Introduction to Java*, which she soon switched to *Intro to Computer Science* with a professor she had heard good things about. On her first day of class, she recognized that she was the only female. She matches her feelings with her critical consciousness that computer science is dominated by male representation. She texted me as she was waiting for her class to start (Fig. 6.1).

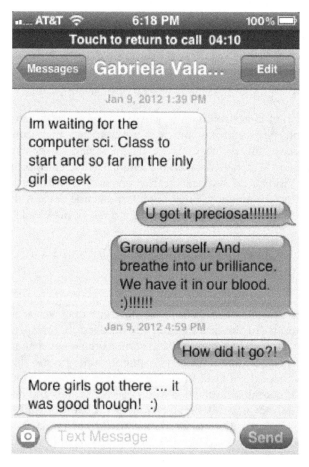

Fig. 6.1 Itzel's critical consciousness on the first day of computer science class at UCSC

When Itzel stepped onto UCLA's campus for the first time since her 3rd-grade field trip, I walked with her. We went to Boelter Hall[1] together and waited for the rest of the group to show up. I dismissed myself and we shared public transportation back home after the day's sessions at UCLA had come to an end. We debriefed about our day, and she felt confident enough to continue her journey through CENS that summer. And we continued to tell each other about our academic and personal journeys. She told me once that I was like her "second mother." This is why I do what I do. Because I know that my connection to educational justice in the faces and hearts of people is a connection that is delicately sealed across boundaries of institutional structures. "It has been an honor to walk beside you, Itzel," I told her then, "We learn so from each other."

We continued to have this connection, despite the physical distance that may separate us. Like Elmer said at one of our workshops after his and Itzel's experience at the UCLA Raza Conference, we maintain connections to people who share a common experience across space. When she texted "so far im the inly [*sic*] girl eeek," I reminded her to "ground" herself, like a tree does into the earth. A herd of bison can come to try to run a grounded one over, but the roots remain, grabbing into the earth like hands digging fingers into the dirt. I reminded her to return her mind from what may be a state of anxiety with inconsistent, shallow breaths. Developing a relationship with our bodies in a way that helps us live through moments of difficulty can help us remember our brilliance. Our ancestors were also creative scholars, so darnos a respetar means we give honor to our minds, hearts, livers, voices, bodies, and spirits while critiquing the colonial forces that deny entrance to our dignity. I'm not sure what Itzel perceived of the above five-line text I sent her. But I did make sure to let her know that I trusted her scholarship.

I often speak figuratively. This way of communication follows a discourse that my family uses with dichos like the ones I've sprinkled throughout this dissertation. I find it useful to use figurative language as well because it keeps the space open to interpretation, as Itzel may see fit for her experience. I remember the words and actions of my parents that have taught me how to darme a respetar. This represents a cultural heritage that was passed down from our forebears. I make palpable the connections to the past in the present for the future. My discourse dances with time.

Itzel's introduction to computer science class equipped her with some skills and consciousness that she continued to share with her community of El Sereno. The following email exchange demonstrates an example of the type of sharing of knowledge that she fed to us, directed to groups of students that she maintains as a part of her journey (Fig. 6.2).

Her connections to her schooling community remain close. Her foresight demonstrated a sense of care that extends a sense of "make-you-feel good" critique of cultural studies. Itzel is interested in helping Mr. Adams deliver content knowledge to his students in a way that students will "understand programming more." I am not sure whether she joined an organization that would maintain her connections to cultural science on her university campus. She has, however, expressed interest in joining our MEChA journey to Tenochtitlán and Teotihuacán this summer. Our goal is to explore the creative science of our shared ancestral history as we excavate with archaeologists, paint and mold with long-time generations of artists, and explore our ancestral foodway cultivation.

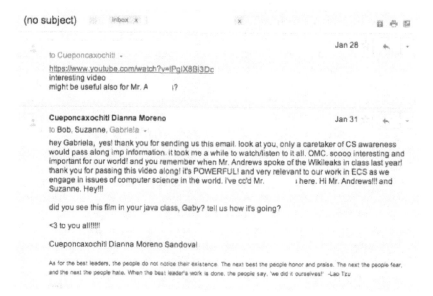

Fig. 6.2   Itzel spreading seeds of intellectual merit in computer science

6.3   EDIBLE CAMPUS, EDIBLE NEIGHBORHOOD

The People's Garden, The Planting Festival, and the Annual Healthy Start Fair are three examples of community involvement that has extended beyond the walls of the classroom. Although it has been a challenge to set up a consistent collaboration between the three classes on these projects that feed food-justice initiatives in our schooling neighborhood, each class works toward preparing student-produced artifacts that would serve the larger goals of our vision to mobilize ancestral knowledge, computer science learning, and student inquiry para el vivir comunitario. For example, the LDIR class has taken the DietSens data from last year to include in a Saturday community presentation at a local junior college.

Our collaborative meetings cultivated a theoretical approach to our collective action. We read the work of Anibal Quijano (2000) and Ramon Grosfuguel (2004, 2008) as we examined the ways in which our collective action was informed by scholarship that re-affirmed our critical consciousness about re-constituting a positive cultural identity as an academic practice for communal health. Kevin shared some of the visions that the Tree Club expressed at one of their meetings for building an edible campus, an edible neighborhood, as a collective effort toward food sovereignty in our community.

In her talk on food sovereignty and sustainability at California State Polytechnic University at Pomona, Winona LaDuke (2010) set up the stage for her audience to "imagine a post-petroleum society" by "remember[ing] who we are" as indigenous peoples to a place on the earth and cultivating our relationships to the land we inhabit. She reminds us about the "arrogance of Empire" that names sacred mountains after "small men," for example, Mt. Mckay, which was once called the "place where the thunder beings rest" in her native language. She questions the practice of naming landscapes after colonizing men: "What does this do to our collective psyche, a nation's spirit, and our relationship to the land?"

Winona raised a point about questioning our energy sources as well. She gave the example of her community that once spent one-fourth of its income on energy that was outsourced. With food sovereignty in mind, her community brought in turbines that operated with the class-four wind that passes through their reservation. "We would not be the ones that people bet on," LaDuke said of her people, who suffered from high unemployment rates and dire mental and physical health conditions. "You just gotta be long-haul people. Pace yourselves. Be tough. Be committed." Winona continued to break down current food consumption trends in the United States: "Our average meal travels 1,400 miles from farmer to table." Sharing the Tree People's idea, LaDuke suggested turning lawns into gardens: "A 10 X 20-square-foot space can generate $750 worth of food, but more than that, one develops a relationship to the land that is social and spiritual, surpassing anything that we can quantify as we decouple our food system from oil." She pushed us to "get used to it early by decolonizing children's taste buds."

On planting corn on her reservation, the community noticed that "the corn remembered the land they came from. The growth of corn helped reconcile, heal our community" through the collective effort of returning to a dignified collective identity and agency.

6.4   LIMITATIONS

One of the most common critiques of embodying an ancestral approach to living today is the danger of romanticizing the past, as if the ancestors "back then" lived more peacefully, with greater insight, and better than today, in a utopian paradise of living, learning, and dying. This is far from the truth. We can also observe colonial practices before European contact in the Western hemisphere, with the rise of the war-like society of the Mexica, a patriarchal (Martinez-Cruz, 2011) society that ostracized women's contributions to medical practices. Also, the Mexica were known as a conquering society that sought to "take over" neighboring lands, demanding a tribute in return. The difference between that type of domination and what we experience now is quite obvious. We are now witnesses to dominant forces that preclude cultural genocide under a neoliberalist state.

This dissertation adopts the "language of critique and possibility" (Aronwitz & Giroux, 1993) as a means to reveal the possibilities that exist for educational excellence. Yet the study did not detail all the challenges that surfaced along the way; I stayed away from building up depressing news, the harsh reality of public schooling climates in the United States, particularly in urban centers. Instead, I focused on a story of resistance, and, by doing so, perhaps the details about what students are actually resisting have been left out, glossing over the stark realities of urban public schooling in El Sereno.

There is a New Age movement that essentializes indigenous cultures, such as marketing "the peasant look" or mystifying medicinal and spiritual practices of native peoples. This dissertation challenges those who would appropriate other people's cultures as if it were their own. Another approach is participating in native activities with the clear understanding of one's positionality in relation to others and by invitation. There is power in sharing one's knowledge systems, but I essentially agree with Ward Churchill (1994) when he describes all people as "indigenous somewhere" and makes a call for all people to be curious about their own cultural practices, so as to liberate their own people. In the United States, we are standing on land that does not ancestrally match the majority of people living on it mainly due to economic and philosophical notions that lead to physical and cultural genocide because we are pushed to develop societal amnesia. The scope of this dissertation does not address the fine details of my previous statements, which may leave open spaces without critiquing them at length.

Although I consider my positionality as a strength in my research, it may also feel like binding. My participation in computer science has increased my awareness with a critical approach to historicized technology production, while my increased critical consciousness about the historically politicized field of computer science, I see the current state of computer science production more of a *problem* than a *solution*. And because my role as a unique Xicana scholar activist that intimately connects to my schooling community, I am often seen as a role model for the few representations of Mesomerican-descent females in academia. So, did I feed Itzel poison? When is my relationship to my schooling community compromised by the dynamics of power?

My worldview is marbled with the heavy influences of my family, my activism, my scholarship, and my personal experiences on equal footing. One of the most difficult challenges for me (although I've come to enjoy it, too) was to alienate myself during the completion of this dissertation season. Perceiving my writing practice as activism (writivism) has been challenging in the sense that it seems counterintuitive to spend months silently and individually typing away at the keyboard while the garden's weeds grow and the world continues to turn around me, relying on the rest of the community to "hold down the fort," trusting that this writing will help spawn our collective vision of food justice, educational excellence, family communing, and positive cultural identities as academic practices, all feeding el vivir comunitario.

Our plan for the next iteration of participatory action research is a continuation of this work, but with another edge. We hope to have time to collectively write about our experiences, our reflections, and our interpretations. Because the university requires that I be the sole author of this dissertation, it was impossible to make it happen on this round, but we hope that our future work will publish student-led initiatives by the community in which we live and act.

6.5   IMPLICATIONS AND DISCUSSION

In its totality, this work is a historical document that tells the story of a schooling community of practice that walks in beauty[2] on multiple roads that challenge notions of self-respect. In other words, it is not easy to be in the eye of the storm that is public education within neoliberalism. This critical narrative inquiry begins and ends with student inquiry and adult support. It is within the figured world of ancestral computing that students and adults navigated a critical awareness of ancestral praxis within the context of food insecurity in our neighborhood and leveraged computing for social action. This study serves as a working example of how student-led initiatives can inform classroom practices, and how these overlaps between student activism and classroom teacher collaboration can feed larger neighborhood activities within a larger vision of sustainability in neoliberalist times. No study will ever be neatly applicable to another community because every context is different. However, there may be aspects of this study that can transfer into other schooling communities, as such communities may see fit. For example, if a schooling community decides to design a research study around the perceptions of self-image and Hollywood's notions of beauty, students and adult supporters may decide to use open-source venues online to create an application that may be uploaded for use on a number of data collectors.

This study reveals how ancestral praxis and computer science motivate positive cultural identities as academic practices. It contributes to decolonial scholarship in education in that it narrates cultural practices for collective agency and critical computer science production. It models a pathway among three organizational levels of education: student-led organization, classroom practice, and larger schooling community.

6.6   FUTURE VISIONS

When I think about the labor of love that a community of practice engaged with over time, I think about how many lives have been changed. When we see our community as a body of water, we see ripples in every person. When one community member shows bravery, and grows, it marks the way for others to change, too. If one household figures out how to sustain a community garden, they are a resource to every neighborhood. If one child in one household secures a CS career, it is not just that one household that is improved. This healing ripples outward, exponentially.

Consider the lasting change represented in a single teacher, Mr. Adams. When he began participating in our inquiry, he was hesitant, and did not trust his ability to guide students in Computer Science. Now he has stepped into his power as a teacher, and will guide countless students into new understanding about their own proficiencies, seeding his bravery alongside their own. Those students take this confidence home, and may encourage siblings, friends, and parents. Again, it ripples outward.

I see decolonization in the future of the field of computer science, and the methods we use to weave our ancestral knowledge ways with computer science can help us decolonize other fields, STEM and otherwise.

Starting with students, and empowering them to explore, experiment, and harness their own creativity ensures future generations will continue this work, and work like it. We now move into the future, with dignity and hope.

To the Great Mother Earth who held us all, who holds us all, and feeds us, thank you. Thank you for the inspiration to continue this labor of love for the future generations.

NOTES

1. Boelter Hall UCLA is considered the birthplace of ARPANET, the precursor to the Internet ... the room from which the first Internet message originated is in Boelter Hall.
2. I have heard this phrase "walk in beauty" as a Navajo adage.

REFERENCES

Aronowitz, S., & Giroux, H. (1993). *Education still under siege*. Westport, CT: Bergin and Garvey.

Churchill, W. (1994). *Indians are us? Culture and genocide in native North America*. Monroe, ME: Common Courage Press.

Grosfoguel, R. (2004). Race and ethnicity or racialized ethnicities?: Identities within global coloniality. *Ethnicities, 4*(3), 315–336.

Grosfoguel, R. (2008). Latin@s and the decolonization of the US empire in the 21st century. *Social Science Information, 47*(4), 605–622.

LaDuke, W. (2010). *Talk on food sovereignty and sustainability at California State Polytechnic University at Pomona*.

Martinez-Cruz, P. (2011) *Women and knowledge in Mesoamerica: From East L.A. to Anahuac*. Tucson, AZ: University of Arizona Press.

Moreno Sandoval, C. D. (2017). Critical ancestral computing for the protection of Mother Earth. In C. Coulter & M. Jiménez-Silva (Eds.), *Culturally sustaining and revitalizing pedagogies: Language, culture and power* (pp. 25–40). Bingley, UK: Emerald Publishing Limited.

Moreno Sandoval, C. D., Hernández-Saca, D., & Tefera, A. (2017). Intersectional rights of teachers and students in computer science and special education: Implications for urban schooling. *Urban Education*, pp. 1–30.

Moreno Sandoval, C. D., Mojica Lagunas, R., Montelongo, L., & Díaz, M. (2016). Ancestral knowledge systems: A conceptual framework for decolonizing research in social science. *AlterNative: An International Journal of Indigenous Peoples, 12*(1), 18–31.

Quijano, A. (2000). Coloniality of power and eurocentrism in Latin America. *International Sociology, 15*(2), 215–232.

REFERENCES

Aguilar, M. (2009). *The rituals of kindness: The influence of the Danza Azteca tradition of Central Mexico on Chicano Mexcoehuani identity and sacred space* (Unpublished dissertation). Claremont Graduate University.

Anonymous. (2010, August 6). Mapping Los Angeles: El Sereno. *Los Angeles Times*. Retrieved from http://projects.latimes.com/mapping-la/neighborhoods/neighborhood/el-sereno/.

Anyon, J. (1997). *Ghetto schooling: A political economy of urban educational reform*. New York: Teachers College Press, Teachers College, Columbia University.

Anzaldúa, G. E. (1987). *Borderlands: The New Mestiza = La Frontera*. San Francisco: Spinsters/Aunt Lute.

Apple, M. W. (1999) *Official Knowledge: Democratic education in a conservative age*. New York: Routledge.

Aronowitz, S., & Giroux, H. A. (1993). *Education still under siege*. Westport, CT: Bergin and Garvey.

Barrow, L. H. (2010). Encouraging creativity with scientific inquiry. *Creative Education, 1*(1), 1–6.

Barton, A. C., & Tobin, K. (2001). Urban science education. *Journal of Research on Science Teaching, 38*, 843–846.

Bauman, Z. (1996). From pilgrim to tourist—Or a short history of identity. In S. Hall & P. du Gay (Eds.), *Questions of cultural identity* (pp. 18–36). London: Sage.

Behar, R. (1996). *The vulnerable observer: Anthropology that breaks your heart*. Boston, MA: Beacon Press.

© The Editor(s) (if applicable) and The Author(s) 2019
C. D. M. Sandoval, *Ancestral Knowledge Meets Computer Science Education*, Postcolonial Studies in Education,
https://doi.org/10.1057/978-1-137-47520-6

Berdan, F. F., Chance, J. K., Sandstrom, A. R., Stark, B., Taggart, J., & Umberger, E. (2008). *Ethnic identity in Nahua Mesoamerica: The view from archaeology, art history, ethnohistory, and contemporary ethnography.* Salt Lake City, UT: University of Utah Press.

Bonilla-Silva, E. (2001). *White supremacy and racism in the post-civil rights era, Lynne.* Boulder, CO: Rienner.

Boone, E. H. (1994). Aztec pictorial histories: Records without words. In E. H. Boone & W. D. Mignolo (Eds.), *Writing without words: Alternative literacies in Mesoamerica and the Andes* (pp. 50–76). Durham and London: Duke University Press.

Bowles, S., & Gintis, H. (1976). *Schooling in capitalist America: Educational reform and the contradictions of economic life.* New York: Basic Books.

Brown, A. (1992). Design experiments: Theoretical and methodological challenges in creating complex interventions in classroom settings. *The Journal of the Learning Sciences, 2*(2), 141–178.

Buckingham, D. (2008). *Youth, identity, and digital media.* Cambridge, MA: MIT Press.

Burciaga, J. A. (1992). *Drink cultura.* Santa Barbara, CA: Joshua Odell Editions.

Camarrota, J., & Fine, M. (2008). *Revolutionizing education: Youth participatory action research in motion.* New York, NY: Routledge.

Champagne, D. & Abu-Saad, I. (Eds.). (2003). *The future of indigenous people: Strategies for survival and development.* Los Angeles, CA: UCLA American Indian Studies Center.

Chrystos. (1983). I walk in the history of my people. In G. Anzaldúa & C. Moraga (Eds.), *This bridge called my back: Writings by radical women of color.* New York, NY: Kitchen Table.

Churchill, W. (1994). *Indians are us? Culture and genocide in native North America.* Monroe, ME: Common Courage Press.

Churchill, W. (2003). *Acts of rebellion: The ward churchill reader* (pp. 243–244). London: Psychology Press.

Clandinin, D. J., & Connelly, F. M. (1988). Studying teachers' knowledge of classrooms: Collaborative research, ethics and the negotiation of narrative. *The Journal of Educational Thought, 22*(2A), 269–282.

Cleary, L., & Peacock, T. (1998). *Collected wisdom: American Indian education.* Boston: Allyn & Bacon.

Cobb, P., & Hodge, L. (2007). Culture, identity, and equity in the mathematics classroom. In N. S. Nasir & P. Cobb (Eds.), *Improving access to mathematics.* New York: Teachers College Press.

Coleman-Jensen, A., Nord, M., Adams, M., & Carlson, S. (2008). *Household food security in the United States.* Washington, DC: Economic Research Service, United States Department of Agriculture.

Comas-Díaz, L. (2001). *Hispanics, Latinos, or Americanos:* The evolution of identity. *Cultural Diversity and Ethnic Minority Psychology, 7*(2), 115–120.

Comas-Díaz, L. & Greene, B. (1994). *Women of color: Integrating ethnic and gender identities in psychotherapy.* New York: The Guilford Press.

Connelly, F. M., & Clandinin, D. J. (1990). Stories of experience and narrative inquiry. *Educational Researcher, 19*(5), 2–14.

Connelly, F. M., & Clandinin, D. J. (2006). Narrative inquiry. In J. L. Green, G. Camilli, & P. B. Elmore (Eds.), *Handbook of complimentary methods in education research* (pp. 477–487). Washington, DC: American Educational Research Association.

Cowan, P. M. (2007). ¡Adelante! Conectándose al pasado, anhelando el futuro a través del discurso visual latino. *Revista Mexicana de Investigación Educativa, 12*(34), 951–986.

Cruz, C. (2006). Toward an epistemology of a brown body. *International Journal of Qualitative Studies in Education, 14*(5), 657–669.

Cuezalin and Huitzilmazatzin; Xochimecayahualli. Xochiilhuitl Celebration of the flower. March 19, 2011.

Darder, A. (2012). *Culture and power in the classroom.* New York: Routledge.

DataQuest. (2010). Educational Demographics Unit. Retrieved February 16, 2010, from California Department of Education.

DeCuir, J., & Dixson, A. (2004). *"So when it comes out, they aren't that surprised that it is there":* Using critical race theory as a tool of analysis of race and racism in education. *Educational Researcher, 33*(5), 26–31.

Deek, F., Jones, J., McCowan, D., Stephenson, C., & Verno, A. (2003). *A model curriculum for K-12 computer science: Final report of the ACM K12 Task Force Curriculum Committee.* New York, NY: Computer Science Teaching Association.

Delgado Bernal, D. (1998, Winter). Using Chicana feminist epistemology in educational research. *Harvard Educational Review, 68*(4), 555–582.

Delgado Bernal, D., Alejandra Elenes, C., Godinez, F. E., & Villenas, S. (Eds.). (2006). *Chicana/Latina education in everyday life: Feminista perspectives on pedagogy and epistemology.* Albany: State University of New York Press.

Deloria, V., & Wildcat, D. (2001). Power and place: Indian education in America. Golden, CO: American Indian Graduate Center, Fulcrum Resources.

Diaz-Soto, L., Soon, C. C., Villarreal, E., & Campos, E. (2009). Xicana sacred space: A communal circle of compromiso for educational researchers. *Harvard Educational Review, 79*(4), 755–775.

Eastside Café Organizing Committee. (2010, September 19). *Welcome to the Eastside Café!* Available at http://eastsidecafeechospace.blogspot.com/.

Eglash, R. (1999). *African fractals: Modern computing and indigenous design.* New Brunswick, NJ: Rutgers University Press.

Eglash, R. (2001). The race for cyberspace: Information technology in the Black Diaspora. *Science as Culture, 10*(3), 353–374.

Eglash, R. (Producer). (2003). *Culturally situated design tools: Teaching math and computing through culture.* Troy, NY: Rensselaer Polytechnic Institute.

Faye, J. (2001). Subverting the captor's language: Teaching Native science to students of Western science. *American Indian Quarterly, 25*(2), 270–273.

Freire, P. (1970). *Pedagogy of the oppressed.* New York, NY: Herder and Herder.

Froehling, O. (1997). The cyberspace "war of ink and internet" in Chiapas, Mexico. *American Geographical Society, 87*(2), 291–307.

Gallucci, C., Van Lare, M. D., Yoon, I. H., & Boatright, B. (2010). Instructional coaching: Building theory about the role and organizational support for professional learning. *American Educational Research Journal, 47*(4), 919–963.

Gandára, P., & Contreras, F. (2009). *The Latino education crisis: The consequences of failed social policies.* Cambridge, MA and London: Harvard University Press.

Gonzáles, P., & Rodríguez, R. (2005). *Amoxtli san ce tojuan: We are one— nosotros somos uno.* San Fernando, CA: Xicano Records and Film. Wallerstein (1991, 2003).

Goode, J. (2007). If you build teachers, will students come? The role of teachers in broadening computer science learning for urban youth. *Journal of Educational Computing Research, 36*(1), 65–88.

Gramsci, A. (1971). *Selections from the Prison Notebooks of Antonio Gramsci.* New York: International Publishers.

Grande, S. (2004). *Red pedagogy: Native American social and political thought.* New York: Rowman & Littlefield.

Grosfoguel, R. (2004). Race and ethnicity or racialized ethnicities?: Identities within global coloniality. *Ethnicities, 4*(3), 315–336.

Grosfoguel, R. (2008a). *Transmodernity, border thinking, and global coloniality: Decolonizing political economy and postcolonial studies.* Berkeley: University of California.

Grosfoguel, R. (2008b). Latin@s and the decolonization of the US empire in the 21st century. *Social Science Information, 47*(4), 605–622.

Grosfoguel, R. (2010). Epistemic Islamophobia and colonial social sciences. *Human Architecture: Journal of the Sociology of Self-Knowledge.* Berkeley: University of California; Paris: Maison des Sciences de l'Homme (Ahead Publishing House).

Harding, S. G. (1998). *Is science multicultural?: Postcolonialisms, feminisms, and epistemologies.* Bloomington, IN: Indiana University Press.

Holland, D., & Lachiotte, W., Jr. (1998). *Identity and agency in cultural worlds.* Cambridge, MA: Harvard University Press.

hooks, b. (1995). *Killing rage: Ending racism* (1st ed.). New York, NY: H. Holt and Co.

hooks, b. (2000). *Where we stand: Class matters.* New York, NY: Routledge.

Hoopes, J. B. (2009). *Acceptance and interpersonal functioning: Testing mindfulness models of empathy.* Austin, TX: The University of Texas at Austin.

Horkheimer, M. (1982). *Critical theory.* New York: Seabury Press.

Howard, T. (2003). Culturally relevant pedagogy: Ingredients for critical teacher reflection. *Theory into Practice, 42*(3), 195–202.

Huanacuni Mamani, F. (2010). *Buen Vivir/ Vivir Bien Filosofía, políticas, estrategias y experiencias regionales andinas.* Lima, Peru: Coordinadora Andina de Organizaciones Indígenas—CAOI.

Hughes, T. P. (1987). The evolution of large technological systems. In W. Bijker, T. Hughes, & T. Pinch (Eds.), *The social construction of technological systems.* Cambridge: Massachusetts Institute of Technology.

Inden, R. (1990). *Imagining India.* Oxford: Blackwell.

Johnston, A. (2007). Demythologizing or dehumanizing? A response to settlage and the ideals of open inquiry. *Journal of Science Teacher Education, 19*(1), 11–13.

Kahn, R. V. (2010). *Critical pedagogy, ecoliteracy, and planetary crisis: The ecopedagogy movement.* New York: Peter Lang.

Karttunen, F. (1982). Nahua history. In G. Collier et al. (Eds.), *Inca and Aztec states, 1400–1800: Anthropology and history (studies in anthropology)* (pp. 395–417). New York: Academic Press.

Karttunen, F. (1992). *An analytical dictionary of Nahuatl.* Norman, OK: University of Oklahoma Press.

Kelly, A. (2004). Design research in education: Yes, but is it methodological? *Journal of the Learning Sciences, 13*(1), 115–128.

Kincheloe, J. L., & McLaren, P. L. (1994). Rethinking critical theory and qualitative research. In N. K. Denzin & Y. S. Lincoln (Eds.), *Handbook of qualitative research* (pp. 138–157). Thousand Oaks, CA: Sage.

Kirchhoff, P. (1943). *Mesoamerica: Sus límites geográficos, composición étnica y caracteres culturales.* México City: Escuela nacional de antropoligía e historia sociedad de alumnus.

Kirkpatrick, S., McIntyre, L., & Potestio, M. (2010). Child hunger and long-term adverse consequences for health. *Archives of Pediatrics & Adolescent Medicine, 164*(8), 754–762.

LaDuke, W. (2010). *Talk on food sovereignty and sustainability at California State Polytechnic University at Pomona.*

Lareau, A. (2003). *Unequal childhoods: Class, race, and family life* (2nd ed.). Berkeley: University of California Press.

Lawrence-Lightfoot, S. (1994). *I've known rivers: Lives of loss and liberation.* Reading, MA: Addison-Wesley.

Leban S., & McLaren P. (2010). Revolutionary critical pedagogy: The struggle against the oppression of neoliberalism—A conversation with Peter McLaren.

In S. Macrine, P. McLaren & D. Hill (Eds.), *Revolutionizing pedagogy. Marxism and education*. New York: Palgrave Macmillan.

Lenhart, A. (2010). *Teens, cell phones and texting*. Washington, DC: Pew Research Center Publications.

Lewin, K. (1946). Action research and minority problems. *Journal of Social Issues, 2*(4), 34–46.

Lindsey, D. B., & MacDonnell, L. (2011). The inside-out approach. *Journal of Staff Development, 32*(1), 34–38.

López-Austin, A. (1980). *Cuerpo humano e ideología. Las concepciones de los antiguos nahuas*. Mexico City: Universidad Nacional Autónoma de México, Instituto de Investigaciones Antropológicas.

Lomas, J. (2007). The in-between world of knowledge brokering. *British Medical Journal, 334*, 129–132.

Maffie, J. (2005). *Internet encyclopedia of philosophy*. Aztec Philosophy. Available at https://www.iep.utm.edu/aztec/.

Magaloni Kerpel, D. (2012). *Los colores del nuevo mundo. Artistas, materiales y la creación del códice florentino*. Mexico City: Universidad Nacional Autónoma de México.

Mander, J. (1992). *In the absence of the sacred: The failure of technology and the survival of the Indian Nations*. San Francisco, CA: Sierra Club Books.

Margolis, J., Estrella, R., & Goode, J. (2008). *Stuck in the shallow end: Education, race, and computing*. Cambridge, MA: MIT Press.

Marin, G. (2008, February 10). *Los guerreros de la muerte florecida* [Blog].

Marin, G. (2009, February 27). *Pedagogía Tolteca*. Paper presented at the California Association for Bilingual Education Annual Conference, Long Beach, CA. Ward Churchill (2003).

Martin, D. B. (2000). *Mathematics success and failure among African-American youth: The roles of sociohistorical context, community forces, school influence, and individual agency*. Mahwah, NJ: Lawrence Erlbaum.

Martin, D. B. (2007). Mathematics learning and participation in the African American context: The co-construction of identity in two intersecting realms of experience. In N. S. Nasir & P. Cobb (Eds.), *Improving access to mathematics*. New York and London: Teachers College Columbia University.

Martin, D. B. (2009). *Mathematics teaching, learning, and liberation in the lives of black children*. New York: Routledge.

Martin, D. B., & McGee, E. O. (2009). Mathematics literacy for liberation: Reframing mathematics education for African American children. In B. Greer, S. Mukhophadhay, S. Nelson-Barber & A. Powell (Eds.), *Culturally responsive mathematics education* (pp. 207–238). New York: Routledge.

Martínez, E. (2009). *500 years of Chicana women's history, 500 años de la mujer chicana*. New Brunswick, NJ: Rutgers University Press.

Martinez-Cruz, P. (2011). *Women and knowledge in Mesoamerica: From East L.A. to Anahuac.* Tucson, AZ: University of Arizona Press.

Martínez Paradez, D. (1973). *Hunab Kú: Síntesis del pensamiento filosófico maya.* Mexico City: Editorial Orión.

McDermott, R., & Varenne, H. (1995). Culture as disability. *Anthropology & Education Quarterly, 26,* 324–348.

McLaren, P. (1988). Culture or canon? Critical pedagogy and the politics of literacy. *Harvard Educational Review, 58*(2): 213–234.

McLaren, P. (2007). *Life in schools: An introduction to critical pedagogy in the foundations of education.* Boston: Pearson Education.

Mignolo, W. D. (1995). *The darker side of the renaissance: Literacy, territoriality, and colonization.* Ann Arbor: University of Michigan Press.

Milner, H. R. (2011). Culturally relevant pedagogy in a diverse urban classroom. *Urban Review, 43,* 66–89.

Morales, E. (2009, May 29). *Letter of Evo Morales to the continental indigenous summit.* Paper presented at the Continental Summit of Indigenous Peoples, Abya Yala Puno, Peru, La Paz.

Moreno Sandoval, C. D. (2017a). Exploring computer science for bi/multilingual learners: A case study using ancestral knowledge systems as border pedagogy in an East Los Angeles High School Classroom. In Ramirez, P. C., Faltis, C. J., & De Jong, E. J. (Eds.), *Learning from emergent bilingual Latinx learners in K-12: Critical teacher education.* London: Routledge.

Moreno Sandoval, C. D. (2017b). Critical ancestral computing for the protection of Mother Earth. In C. Coulter & M. Jiménez-Silva (Eds.), *Culturally sustaining and revitalizing pedagogies: Language, culture and power* (pp. 25–40). Bingley, UK: Emerald Publishing Limited.

Moreno Sandoval, C. D., Hernández-Saca, D., & Tefera, A. (2017). Intersectional rights of teachers and students in computer science and special education: Implications for urban schooling. *Urban Education,* pp. 1–30.

Moreno Sandoval, C. D., Mojica Lagunas, R., Montelongo, L., & Díaz, M. (2016). Ancestral knowledge systems: A conceptual framework for decolonizing research in social science. *AlterNative: An International Journal of Indigenous Peoples, 12*(1), 18–31.

Morrell, E. (2008). *Critical literacy and urban youth: Pedagogies of access, dissent, and liberation.* New York, NY: Routledge.

Nasir, N. I. S., & Hand, V. (2006). Exploring sociocultural perspectives on race, culture, and learning. *American Educational Research Association, 76*(4), 449–475.

Newcomb, S. (2008). *Pagans in the promised land: Decoding the doctrine of christian discovery.* Golden, CO: Fulcrum Publishing.

Olmeca. (2009). *La contra cultura/counter culture: Pieces of me.* Los Angeles: El Sereno, California.

Omi, M., & Winant, H. (1974, September). *Racial formations in the United States.* London: Scientific American, Nature Publishing Group.

Omi, M., & Winant, H. (1994). *Racial formation in the United States: From the 1960s to the 1990s (critical social thought)* (2nd ed.). New York: Routledge.

Orfield, G., Losen, D., Wald, J., & Swanson, C. B. (2004). *Losing our future: How minority youth are being left behind by the graduation rate crisis.* Cambridge: The Civil Rights Project at Harvard University.

Oxford English Dictionary. (2000). Oxford University Press.

Oxford English Dictionary. (2011). Oxford: Oxford University Press.

Paris, D. (2012). Culturally sustaining pedagogy: A needed change in stance, terminology, and practice. *Educational Researcher, 41*(93), 93–97.

Pew Hispanic Research Center. (2009). *Between two worlds: How young Latinos come of age in America.* http://www.pewhispanic.org/2009/12/11/between-two-worlds-how-young-latinos-come-of-age-in-america/. Accessed May 8, 2011.

The Philosophy of Movimiento Estudiantil Chicano de Aztlan. (1969). Available at http://www.cwu.edu/~mecha/documents/phyiosophy.pdf.

Quijano, A. (1991). Colonialidad y Modernidad/Racionalidad. *Perú Indígena, 13*(29), 11–20. Lima, Peru: Instituto Indigenista Peruano.

Quijano, A. (1998). Colonialidad, Poder, Cultura y Conocimiento en América Latina. In *Anuario Mariateguiano, IX*(9), 113–122. Lima: Amauta.

Quijano, A. (2000). Coloniality of Power and Eurocentrism in Latin America. *International Sociology, 15*(2), 215–232.

Rennera, A., Brown, M., Stiens, G., & Burton, S. (2010). A reciprocal global education? Working towards a more humanizing pedagogy through critical literacy. *Intercultural Education, 21*(1), 41–54.

Rogers, J., Bertrand, M., Freelon, R., & Fanelli, S. (2011). *California educational opportunity.* Los Angeles, CA: UCLA's Institute for Democracy, Education, and Access.

Rosser, S. V. (1995). *Teaching the majority: Breaking the gender barrier in science, mathematics, and engineering.* New York, NY: Teachers College Press.

Roth, W. M. (2004). Identity as dialectic: Re/making self in urban school. *Mind, Culture, and Activity, 11*(1), 48–69.

Sandoval, C. (2000). *Methodology of the oppressed.* Minneapolis: University of Minnesota Press.

Sapolsky, R. (2005). The influence of social hierarchy on primate health. *Science, 308*(5722), 648–652.

Sfard, A., & Prusak, A. (2005). Telling identities: In search of an analyitic tool for investigating learning as a culturally shaped activity. *Educational Researcher, 34*(4), 14–22.

Smith, L. T. (1999). *Decolonizing methodologies: Research and indigenous peoples.* London: Zed Books.

Solorzano, D. G., & Yosso, T. J. (2002). A critical race counterstory of race, racism, and affirmative action. *Equity & Excellence in Education, 35*, 155–168. University of Massachusetts School of Education Journal.

Somé, S. (1999). *The spirit of intimacy: Ancient teachings in the ways of relationships.* Green Forest, AR: Newleaf.

Somé, S. (2000). *The spirit of intimacy: Ancient African teachings in the ways of relationships* (1st ed.). New York: William Morrow Paperbacks.

Steele, C. (1997). A threat in the air: How stereotypes shape intellectual identity and performance. *American Psychologist, 52*(6), 613–629.

Strauss, A., & Corbin, J. (1990). *Basics of qualitative research: Grounded theory procedures and techniques.* Newbury Park, CA: Sage.

Suárez-Orozco, C., & Suárez-Orozco, M. M. (1995). *Transformations: Immigration, family life, and achievement motivation among Latino adolescents.* Redwood City, CA: Stanford University Press.

Textor, R. B. (1967). *A cross-cultural summary.* New Haven, CT: HRAF Press.

Tornatzky, L. G., Macias, E. E., & Jones, S. (2002). *Latinos and information technology: The promise and the challenge.* Claremont, CA: The Tomás Rivera Policy Institute.

Turkle, S. (2011). *Alone together: Why we expect more from technology and less from each other.* New York, NY: Basic Books.

Tyack, D. B. (1974). *The one best system: A history of American urban education.* Cambridge, MA: Harvard University Press.

Utting, I., Cooper, S., K¨olling, M., Maloney, J., & Resnick, M. (2010, November). Alice, greenfoot and scratch—A discussion. *ACM Transactions on Computing Education, 10*(4), Article 17, 11 pages. http://doi.acm.org/10.1145/1868358.1868364.

Valenzuela, A. (1999). *Subtractive schooling: U.S. Mexican youth and the politics of caring.* Albany, NY: State University of New York Press.

Vaughan, D. (2002). Signals of interpretive work: The role of culture in a theory of practical action. In K. A. Cerulo (Ed.), *Culture in mind: Toward a sociology of culture and cognition* (pp. 28–54). New York: Routledge.

Ventana A Mi Comunidad is a series of YouTube videos that are produced by the Secretaría de Educación Pública in Mexico. "Serie de videos Ventana a mi Comunidad. Una producción de Videoservicios Profesionales SA de CV para la Coordinación General de Educación Intercultural y Bilingüe de la Secretaría de Educación Pública, México."

Viesca, C. (2003). Medicine across cultures: History and practice of medicine in non-western cultures. In H. Selin (Ed.), *Science across cultures: The history of non-western science book* (Vol. 3). Berlin: Springer.

Vygotski, L. S. (1978). *Mind and society: The development of higher psychological processes.* Cambridge, MA: Harvard University Press.

Wenger, E. (2010). Communities of practice and social learning systems: The career of a concept. In C. Blackmore (Ed.), *Social learning systems and communities of practice* (Vol. x, Part III, pp. 179–198). London: Springer-Verlag.

Wilcox, D. C., Wilcox, B. J., & Poon, L. W. (2011). Centenarian studies: Important contributors to our understanding of the aging process and longevity. *Current Gerontology and Geriatrics Research, 2010,* 1–6.

Woodson, C. G. (1933/1990). *The mis-education of the Negro.* Trenton, NJ: Africa World Press.

Wortham, S. (2007). The interdependence of social identification and learning. *American Educational Research Journal, 41*(3), 715–750.

Yosso, T. (2005). Whose culture has capital? A critical race theory discussion of community cultural wealth. *Race Ethnicity and Education, 8*(1), 69–91.

Yosso, T., & Solórzano, D. (2006, March). *Leaks in the Chicana and Chicano Educational Pipeline* (Latino Policy and Issues Brief, No. 13). UCLA Chicano Studies Research Center.

INDEX

GPSR Compliance
The European Union's (EU) General Product Safety Regulation (GPSR) is a set
of rules that requires consumer products to be safe and our obligations to
ensure this.

If you have any concerns about our products, you can contact us on

ProductSafety@springernature.com

In case Publisher is established outside the EU, the EU authorized
representative is:

Springer Nature Customer Service Center GmbH
Europaplatz 3
69115 Heidelberg, Germany